Barbie™

A RARE BEAUTY

Sandi Holder

Published by

Krause Publications, a division of F+W Media, Inc.
700 East State Street • Iola, WI 54990-0001
715-445-2214 • 888-457-2873
www.krausebooks.com

To order books or other products call toll-free 1-800-258-0929
or visit us online at www.krausebooks.com or www.Shop.Collect.com

Cover photography by Kris Kandler

Library of Congress Control Number: 2010923673

ISBN-13: 978-1-4402-1279-6
ISBN-10: 1-4402-1279-1

Designed by Rachael Knier
Edited by Paul Kennedy

Printed in China

Dedication

I DEDICATE THIS BOOK TO MY BROTHER LARRY who passed away in 2003. There is not a day that goes by that I don't think of how lucky I am to have had a brother like you. Your life ended too quickly and even if we are in different places now our hearts are connected. Our endless conversations about your love for the Beatles and my love for Barbie are memories I hold so close.

Acknowledgements

I FEEL VERY GRATEFUL that I have a job which has allowed me to meet some of the most wonderful people in the world, experience the greatest friendships ever, and travel to so many great places. There are so many people who have helped me make my dream a reality. Space makes it impossible to name everyone here. If I forget to mention you, I apologize. Please know that your help and friendship are appreciated

Special thanks to my parents George and Joan Schlesinger for being the greatest parents ever; for giving me endless love, advice and support. My parents are my role models, heroes and examples of how hard work does pay off.

To my children: Jessica, Josh and Jenna who have been so understanding of the long hours I have to put into running this business. Thank you for having the utmost patience explaining what your mom does for a living and answering the million of questions associated with the explanation. To Krystle Zoe and Savanah, your endless love and enthusiasm brighten my day. We are so blessed having such an amazing family.

To Cary for all your unconditional love and support; to my sister Nancy who is an endless wealth of knowledge and who can make sense of any situation; niece Jennifer, brother Ed, sons-in-law Michael and Joey, grandchildren Karelli, Sammy and Michael-Joshua who give me endless hours of laughter and love.

Jon Rodriguez, without you, Doll Attic would not be where it is today. Your loyalty and dedication is appreciated every day. Thank you for being so attentive to detail and helping the business grow. You will always remain a part of the Doll Attic family. To Heidi Chung, my assistant, who does an exceptional job of managing Doll Attic when I am away. Thank you for helping on this project and giving me 100% every day. Doll Attic is lucky to have you and I appreciate all you do.

To Michael Bustillos who not only helped me get "those guns" and is the best fitness trainer ever, but also challenged me to heights I never thought possible. Having you as a best friend means the world to me. Underground Fitness, Union City, Calif., has become my second home. Thank you to the Bustillos family for making me a part of your family.

To my friends and fellow Barbie doll dealers Joe Blitman and Kevin Mulligan, thank you for all your support. Thanks Joe for always having time to answer my questions throughout the years. Special thanks to Jef, Lorraine, Shawn, George and Lisa for your love and friendship and helping me live some of the best memories ever.

Special thanks to my friends at F+W Media for giving me this opportunity to share what I love. Paul Kennedy, designer Rachael Knier and photographer Kris Kandler were awesome to work with.

Through this journey, I have learned being the largest Barbie doll dealer doesn't mean you will be the best. I have learned that doing your best each and everyday is what's important.

U.S. Issued Side part American Girl wearing Sears Exclusive, Pink Formal.

Japanese Side Part American Girl in European Exclusive, Midnight Pink.

Contents

A RARE
BEAUTY

Life is what happens while you're making plans for something else. So it was for Sandi Holder who planned on being a nurse, but life had other plans.

From the ER to Barbie's Dream House

Life's twists fuels Holder's passion

SHARON KORBECK VERBETEN

Barbie's Best Friend Award, presented to Holder at the 2006 Barbie National Convention.

ALTHOUGH SHE'S BEEN A FIXTURE IN THE BARBIE DOLL WORLD for almost two decades, Sandi Holder's road to prominence wasn't paved with pink boxes, pilgrim heels and Ponytails. It started, interestingly enough, in the emergency room. In the late 1980s, Holder, owner of Sandi Holder's Doll Attic in Union City, Calif., was working in a hospital emergency room—with dreams of becoming a pediatric intensive care nurse—when fate intervened. When her young son fell seriously ill, Holder's career path changed. "I had to think of something I could do to generate income and be at home with my children," she said.

Holder already had a deep-seated love of Barbie dolls—she had grown up enamored with a brunette Bubblecut wearing the fashion outfit Red Flare. "Barbie represented a very familiar and happy time in my life," she recalled. "I had such good times playing with Barbie. What better outlet than to remember things that were pleasant to you?"

Immersing herself in all things Barbie seemed a perfect antidote to the challenges in her life, so she thought she'd try her hand at selling vintage dolls, clothing and accessories. She began attending doll shows, buying duplicates and assessing the market. "It basically started as a hobby," Holder said. Her venture started with two plastic milk crates in her garage, which she'd fill with vintage Barbie items she'd find at doll

PLEASE DO NOT TOUCH DISPLAY

What fun! A Barbie
dollhouse filled
with favorites.

shows, through advertising or through serendipity. "It wasn't hard [to find inventory], but it wasn't easy," she said. "I had to peruse through many venues."

One of those venues, Holder recalled gleefully, brought her to a woman's house that was piled floor to ceiling with garbage. The owner had told her she had some Barbie dolls, but Holder remained wary...until the woman brought out two small, but tattered, trunks.

"Inside the trunk was a pristine #1 Ponytail Barbie doll wearing Gay Parisienne," Holder said. "That was probably one of my most exciting finds."

After lots of legwork and laying the groundwork for her business, Holder established her Doll Attic in a storefront in the San Francisco Bay area in 1989. "I knew after each list was progressively growing that things were going in the right direction," said Holder, a mother of three grown children.

Those "lists" detailed the vintage dolls she offered for sale. Her first list—compiled in 1990—was 13 pages long and listed 42 dolls. And prices were much different than today. A #4 Brunette Ponytail Barbie doll was selling for $250; Fashion Queens were only $30.

Holder based her prices on what she felt the market would bear. "I gauged it on what I felt was fair market value," she said. "Each list got bigger; it basically was a success; the clientele grew, and I developed a lot of great relationships with the customers. It just kind of evolved."

Holder's business continued to evolve; by the late 1990s, she had acquired a Barbie auction business and held her first auction by phone in 1999. "It was extremely successful. It lasted until 2:30 a.m." she said. "I was just amazed."

Today, auctions are a mainstay of her business. She holds two each year, showcasing some of the rarest Barbie items. "The auction caters to every level of collector. Every auction brings so much to the table," she said.

The success of her auctions is evident in her achieving the record selling price for a Barbie doll—at a 2006 auction, Holder sold a #1 Blond Ponytail in pink silhouette dress box for more than $25,000. "That was an absolutely pristine, untouched doll," Holder said.

Doll Attic has expanded into a "multifaceted operation"—retail store, party venue (for little girls' birthday parties), auction house and museum. The latter opened after a Barbie museum in Palo Alto, Calif., shut its doors—and Holder decided to fill the void. To showcase her vast collection in the best surroundings, she hired staff from Disney and Pixar Studios to bring her vision for the museum to life.

Showcasing the best of vintage and new dolls, the museum gives visitors a peek inside the world of Barbie—one Holder has embraced wholeheartedly for 20 years.

A visitor finds that passion for all things Barbie at Sandi Holder's Doll Attic, which is a long way from that emergency room so many years ago. Yet Holder, who was named Mattel's first Dealer of the Year in 2004 and was the 2006 recipient of Barbie's Best Friend Award given by Mattel designer Carol Spencer, has no regrets of turning her back on the medical field.

"I think I have a really cool job," she said. "I feel I play Santa Claus 365 days of the year.

"I have met some of the most incredible people that I would not have met had it not been for Barbie. The friendships—that's what keeps me doing what I'm doing."

All auction values throughout book are from Doll Attic sales.
For more information on Sandi Holder's
Doll Attic, visit www.dollattic.com.

Ruth and Elliot Handler with Barbie doll, around 1961.

Barbie's Legendary Aura

Taking a Brand to Heart

SHARON KORBECK VERBETEN

*S*HE IS US—AND WE ARE HER. That affinity—that strong emotional connection—is likely the main reason the Barbie doll has become a successful global brand and a cultural icon for more than 50 years.

In the toy world, consumer tastes are fickle, and the stock on shop shelves is ever-changing. Few toys enjoy popularity for more than one or two years. An enduring few may become household names and last for 10, maybe 20 years. But rarely does a toy property endure half a century.

That's why Mattel's Barbie doll—which had a tentative start in 1959 but an eventual and steady rise—has come to occupy its own rarified air in the world of toys. Say the word "Barbie" and nothing more need be said; everyone knows to whom you refer. And Barbie is indeed one of the world's most familiar, and revered, brands.

In the world of toys—and in pop culture—the Barbie brand is evergreen. And despite fluctuations in its image and popularity over five decades, it retains a cachet other toymakers can only dream of for their lines.

What's Mattel's secret to attaining such status for a mere plaything? Sure, product quality, market adaptability and viable marketing all play a role. But the real secret to Barbie's success lies in the power of nostalgia and emotion.

Modeled here by
#6 Blond Ponytail Barbie doll,
Apple Print Sheath.

"Barbie touches so many aspects of a girl's psyche from adventure to independence to dreams of aspirations," wrote Gene Del Vecchio, author of Creating Ever-Cool: A Marketer's Guide to a Kid's Heart, "that the emotional connections with the Barbie brand run deep."

Del Vecchio, a marketing expert, was speaking about the synergy the doll has with its owners that has echoed true for five decades. An emotional connection with a toy is perhaps the best thing a toymaker can hope for; that may be just what Mattel co-founder and Barbie creator Ruth Handler had in mind. Creating that emotional bond didn't happen overnight, however, and it took a healthy dose of change to bring the doll's relationship with its fans to that point. And when change came, it made waves—waves that would prove necessary to the doll's continuing success.

"From the very beginning, Mattel figured out that they needed to keep changing and evolving her style," said Christopher Varaste, a Barbie collector and author from California. In constantly making changes, Mattel paved the way for future dolls and future incarnations. "It paved the way for Barbie to succeed," Varaste added.

But Barbie didn't change solely for the sake of change; she carefully followed—and sometimes predicted—societal trends. "Barbie reflects where we are and where we've just been," said California Barbie dealer and author Joe Blitman. "She changes as we change. She's a perfect mirror; she's constantly being reinvented."

Barbie's reinventions over the years brought with them the loyalty of little girls. Some craved the hair play features of the 1980s dolls. Others coveted the doll's glamorous gowns. Some sought the emotional connections embodied by Barbie, her family and her circle of friends.

With loyalty comes emotion—so it all comes back to emotional connections. And with Barbie, those connections have the power to span generations. Little girls playing with Fashion Fever Barbie dolls today may have mothers who adored their Superstar Barbie in the 1980s, and perhaps grandmothers who owned an original 1961 Bubblecut. "Our parents and grandparents have grown up with it," said Mattel's principal Barbie designer Sharon Zuckerman. "It's been generations of people playing with it...and she's just so beautiful."

Blitman agreed—not only did generations embrace the Barbie doll, all genders did as well. "After 50 years, the doll is a part of so many people's childhoods—male or female," he said. Florida dealer and doll show promoter Marl Davidson noted, "Everybody can relate to her in one way or another, even boys. Their sisters played with them."

No matter the connection—whether a personal, intimate memory or passing recollection—the Barbie name remains ingrained in the psyches of several generations. As Del Vecchio states in his book, "Even though the day may come when children outgrow the functional benefits of your brand, the feelings they have toward it will remain, buried deep within their adult psyches. Then, years later when these adults have children of their own, they will come back. They will remember the relationship."

And that's what Mattel has counted on, and thrived on. Today's adults are avid collectors—fueling the secondary market for vintage dolls and engendering a love of the new dolls in their children and grandchildren. And so the circle of creating an "evergreen,"—or what Del Vecchio calls an "Ever-Cool"—brand continues.

After more than 50 years, Barbie remains ingrained in the pop culture consciousness.

As Blitman aptly said, "When you've been around that long, you take on a legendary aura. You become a touchstone."

Every dream — even a little girl's wedding day — was possible with Barbie doll.

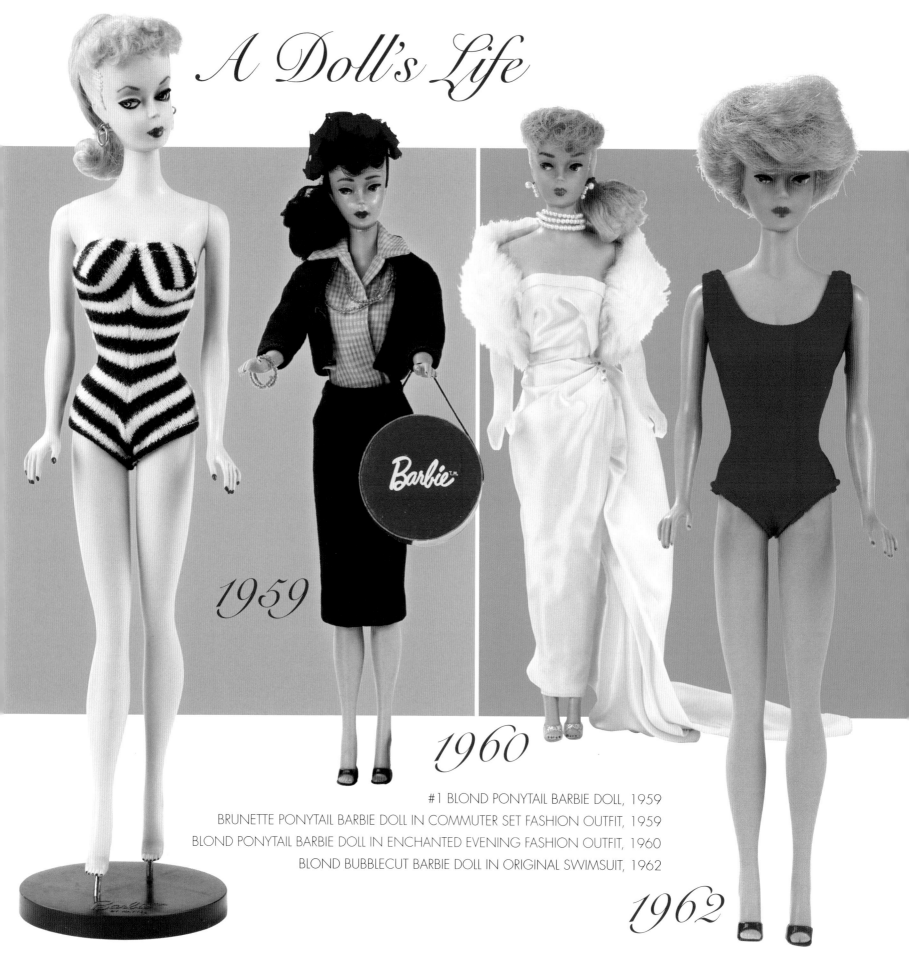

A Doll's Life

1959

1960

1962

#1 BLOND PONYTAIL BARBIE DOLL, 1959
BRUNETTE PONYTAIL BARBIE DOLL IN COMMUTER SET FASHION OUTFIT, 1959
BLOND PONYTAIL BARBIE DOLL IN ENCHANTED EVENING FASHION OUTFIT, 1960
BLOND BUBBLECUT BARBIE DOLL IN ORIGINAL SWIMSUIT, 1962

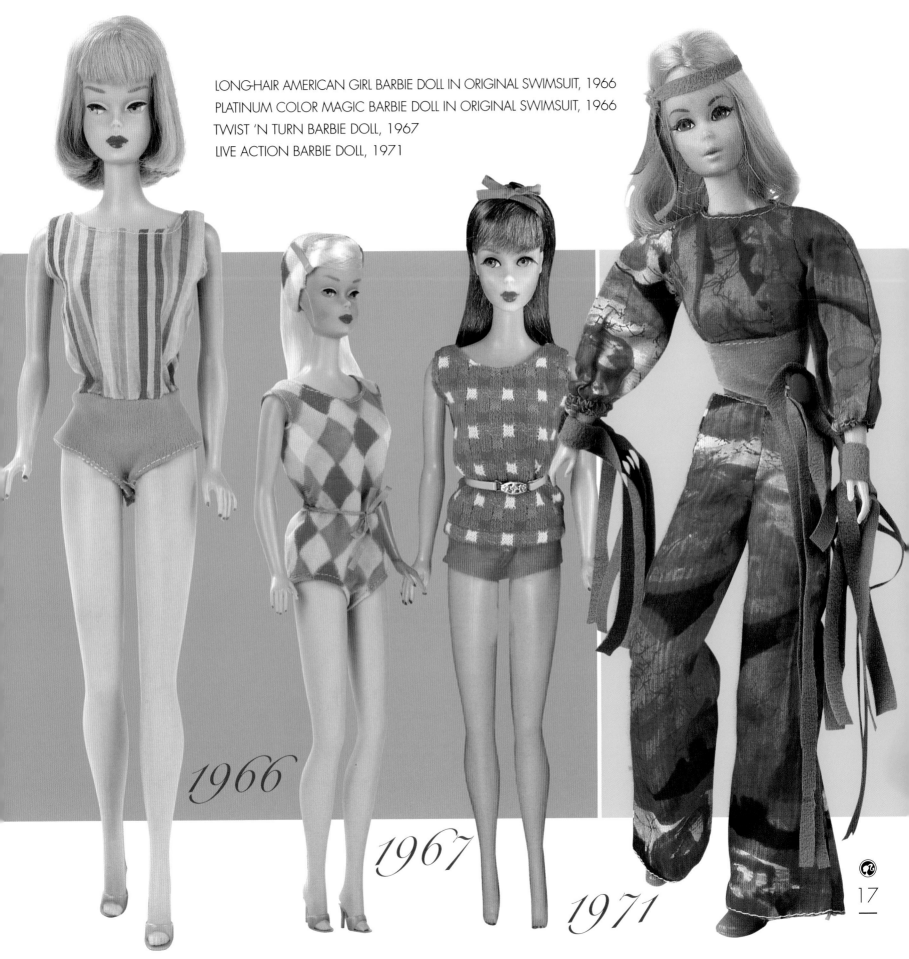

LONG-HAIR AMERICAN GIRL BARBIE DOLL IN ORIGINAL SWIMSUIT, 1966
PLATINUM COLOR MAGIC BARBIE DOLL IN ORIGINAL SWIMSUIT, 1966
TWIST 'N TURN BARBIE DOLL, 1967
LIVE ACTION BARBIE DOLL, 1971

1966

1967

1971

17

1977

SUPERSTAR BARBIE DOLL, 1977
BLACK BARBIE DOLL, 1980
ROCKER BARBIE DOLL, LEADER OF THE ROCKERS, 1986
BOB MACKIE GOLD BARBIE DOLL, 1990

1986

1980

1990

18

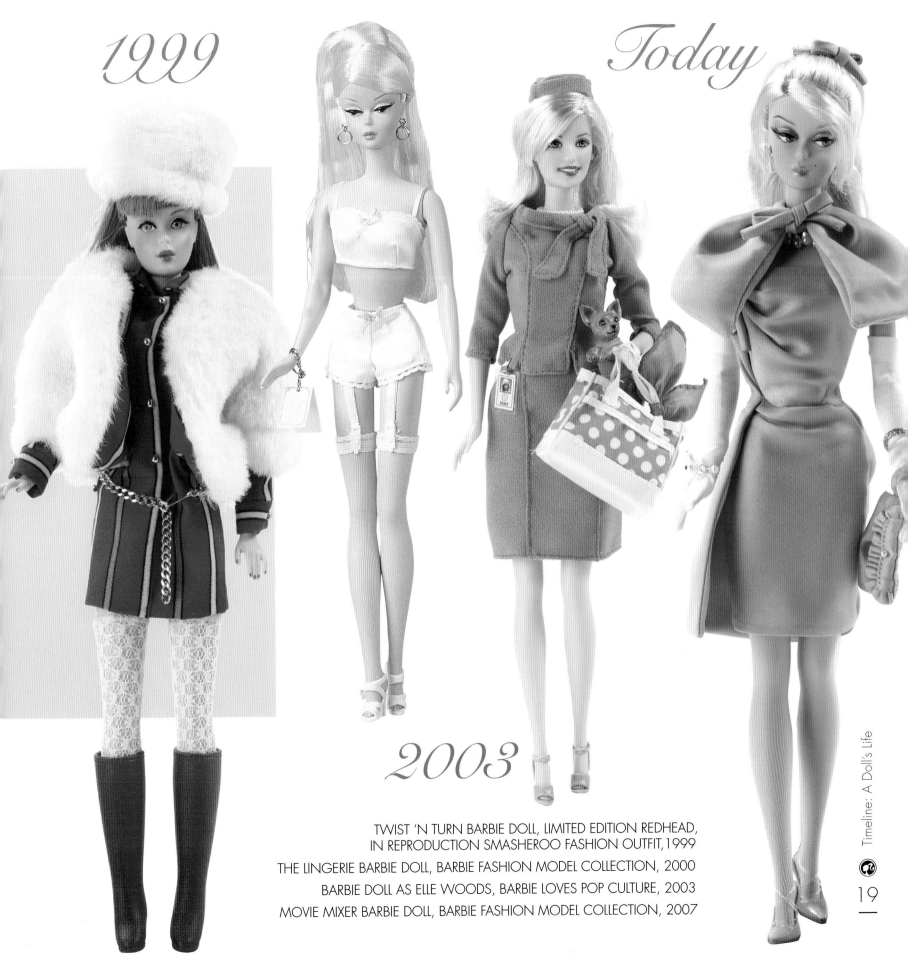

1999

Today

2003

TWIST 'N TURN BARBIE DOLL, LIMITED EDITION REDHEAD,
IN REPRODUCTION SMASHEROO FASHION OUTFIT, 1999
THE LINGERIE BARBIE DOLL, BARBIE FASHION MODEL COLLECTION, 2000
BARBIE DOLL AS ELLE WOODS, BARBIE LOVES POP CULTURE, 2003
MOVIE MIXER BARBIE DOLL, BARBIE FASHION MODEL COLLECTION, 2007

The Handler family at home in California: Ruth, Elliot, Barbara and Ken. The children gained fame as the namesakes of two of the most recognized dolls ever created.

Schlesinger Library, Radcliffe Institute, Harvard University

CHAPTER 1

In the Beginning

Handler Proves Women have Choices

A SULTRY LOOK, AN ENVIABLE FIGURE AND THAT PERKY PONYTAIL. Few dolls are as unmistakably identifiable—or as coveted—as the very first Barbie doll.

There's no disputing that the first Barbie doll was distinctive. In an era of one-dimensional paper dolls and cherubic baby dolls, Mattel's Barbie doll was sophisticated and full of possibilities. Creator and Mattel co-founder Ruth Handler would have it no other way. Barbie was to become the vinyl body through which were projected the imaginations and dreams of every child who played with her.

"My whole philosophy of Barbie was that through the doll, the little girl could be anything she wanted to be," Handler wrote in her 1994 autobiography, *Dream Doll: The Ruth Handler Story*. "Barbie always represented the fact that a woman has choices."

First introduced as a teenage fashion model, Barbie has enjoyed more than 80 careers in the past five decades. She's been everything from an Olympic skater, to a paleontologist, to a presidential candidate. She's served in the armed forces and was a Formula 1 racer. Reach for the stars? Barbie did more than that: as an astronaut she rocketed to the stars.

"Over and over I've had it said to me by women that she was much more than a doll for them. She was part of them," Handler told the Associated Press in 1994.

Handler, who died in 2002 at the age of 85, created not only a wonderful toy for little girls, she helped create one of the most popular and prized collectibles in the toy market. A #1 Ponytail Barbie doll in mint condition sold for more than $25,500 at auction in 2003—a staggering amount for a doll that originally sold for $3.

Part of the reason Barbie has reached such amazing value on the secondary market is that over time the doll has become woven into the fabric of our society. Consider that in 1976, as the country celebrated its Bicentennial, Barbie doll was placed in the official "America's Time Capsule" so that future generations would be ensured the pleasure of her acquaintance.

An amazing businesswoman with a relentless entrepreneurial spirit, Ruth Handler confessed to the Los Angeles Times in 1959 she was "a little lost in the home—I'm just not efficient." From left: Elliot, Ruth, Barbara, and Ken at the piano.

It's important to remember that Barbie's birth came in the 1950s, a time when Americans were enjoying the benefits of a strong, postwar economy. Eisenhower was in the White House and Milton Berle was everyone's favorite Uncle on TV. Ben-Hur commanded Best Picture recognition while teen idols like Fabian and Frankie Avalon broke the hearts of untold numbers of teenage girls. Even Alaska and Hawaii were new to the scene, joining the Union in 1959. And in Detroit, new cars featured big, bold tailfins. There was nothing small about the country back then.

In this backdrop the Baby Boom generation took shape, and Barbie doll right along with it.

The inspiration for Barbie came as Handler watched her daughter, Barbara, playing with paper dolls. Barbara and her friends liked to play adult or teenage make-believe with the paper dolls, imagining them in roles as college students, cheerleaders and adults with careers. Handler, who with her husband, Elliot, launched Mattel in 1945, recognized that experimenting with the future from a safe distance through pretend play was an important part of growing up. She also noticed a marketing void and was determined to fill that niche with a three-dimensional fashion doll.

Today, it is difficult to imagine a little girl not owning at least one Barbie doll, so strong is the brand. Even so, Barbie doll is an incredible and improbable success story.

Consider Ruth Handler, the youngest of ten children of Polish immigrants, who was born Nov. 14, 1916, in Denver. Her parents lived in Warsaw when it was occupied by Russia. Her father, Jacob Moskowicz—the name was shortened to Mosko when he arrived at Ellis Island—was a blacksmith by trade. At one point he served in the Russian Army. Only by going AWOL did he escape to the United States.

When Ruth was six months old, her mother underwent surgery. Ruth's sister Sarah, who was 20 years her elder, took her in. For the next 19 years Ruth lived with Sarah and her husband, Louie Greenwald. Sarah and Louie functioned as her parents, while her real parents were more li ake loving grandparents.

Ironically, Ruth Handler didn't like dolls growing up. She never played with them. Instead, she was an admitted tomboy and enjoyed the company of boys rather than girls. She also enjoyed working at the family's drug store and soda fountain more than playing.

"It's not that I never played," Handler wrote in her autobiography.

"I did have a few close girlfriends and I enjoyed hanging around with them. But I was basically a loner. I rarely had lengthy phone conversations or sleepovers like other kids did. I thought 'girl talk' was stupid."

Despite her own interests and far different background, Handler was committed to filling a void she knew existed from watching her daughter play. It took three years to develop the first Barbie, which debuted at New York's American International Toy Fair in 1959. Handler was confident of a successful launch at the show that featured more than 16,000 wholesale and retail buyers from stores worldwide. Barbie, in her now-familiar black-and-white striped swimsuit, heels and sunglasses—and modest $3 retail price—was sure to be a hit.

Only she wasn't.

A *New York Times* article previewing the Toy Fair stated that Mattel's hottest item for the coming year wasn't Barbie but "a yard-long, two-stage plastic rocket which soars to about 200 feet." The article also noted Mattel's new toy guns. Only a couple of paragraphs were dedicated to the new Barbie doll. Toy buyers were also unimpressed. About half of the buyers who saw her wanted nothing to do with the doll. Never before had they seen a doll so completely unlike the baby and toddler dolls popular at the time. Never before had a doll had such a womanly figure. They remained unsure of the doll's potential.

"Ruth, little girls want baby dolls," one buyer said in a story recounted by Handler in her autobiography. "They want to pretend to be mothers."

Handler was crushed. Her baby, as she described Barbie, had been rejected. But Handler was far from defeated.

"One of my strengths is that I do have the courage of my convictions and the guts to take a position, stand up for it, push for it, and make it happen," Handler wrote in her autobiography. "I can be very persuasive in getting others to see the light."

And of course, she did just that. Once in the marketplace, Barbie doll was a runaway hit. She didn't walk off the shelves, she ran. Mattel reportedly sold more than a quarter of a million of the very first Barbie doll. Today, the vast Barbie doll empire is close to a $2 billion a year industry.

Fueled by vision, courage and conviction, Barbie doll has come a long way from Ruth Handler's simple mission to create a toy for her daughter. Today, children and adults alike collect Barbie with passion and delight.

A #1 Barbie doll booklet autographed by Ruth Handler.

Barbie® TEEN-AGE FASHION MODEL

Ruth Handler

MATTEL INTERNATIONAL

© MCMLVIII by Mattel Inc.

Ruth and Elliot Handler, here in 1938, met in Denver when she was 16. Ruth was smitten at first sight, calling her future husband "gorgeous." Later the two teamed up to help create the largest toy company in the world.

Few teams were as successful as Ruth and Elliot Handler, here surveying every little girl's dream — an entire Barbie doll world at Mattel. Together the Handlers revolutionized the toy business, and made millions of children worldwide very happy.

Schlesinger Library, Radcliffe Institute, Harvard University

Barbie doll may be Ruth Handler's most enduring successes, but she was hardly her only one. Here, Ruth examines a collection of Chatty Cathy dolls, the second most popular doll of the 1960s.

Schlesinger Library, Radcliffe Institute, Harvard University (Photo by Maxine Reams, Los Angeles Times)

The youngest of ten children born to Polish immigrant parents, Ruth Handler was fiercely independent with the ability to dream big dreams. She worked tirelessly to have those same traits reflected in Barbie doll, helping to make the doll the most successful toy of all time.

Schlesinger Library, Radcliffe Institute, Harvard University

This pristine #1 Blond Ponytail Barbie doll set a world record when it sold at a Doll Attic auction for $25,527 in 2003.

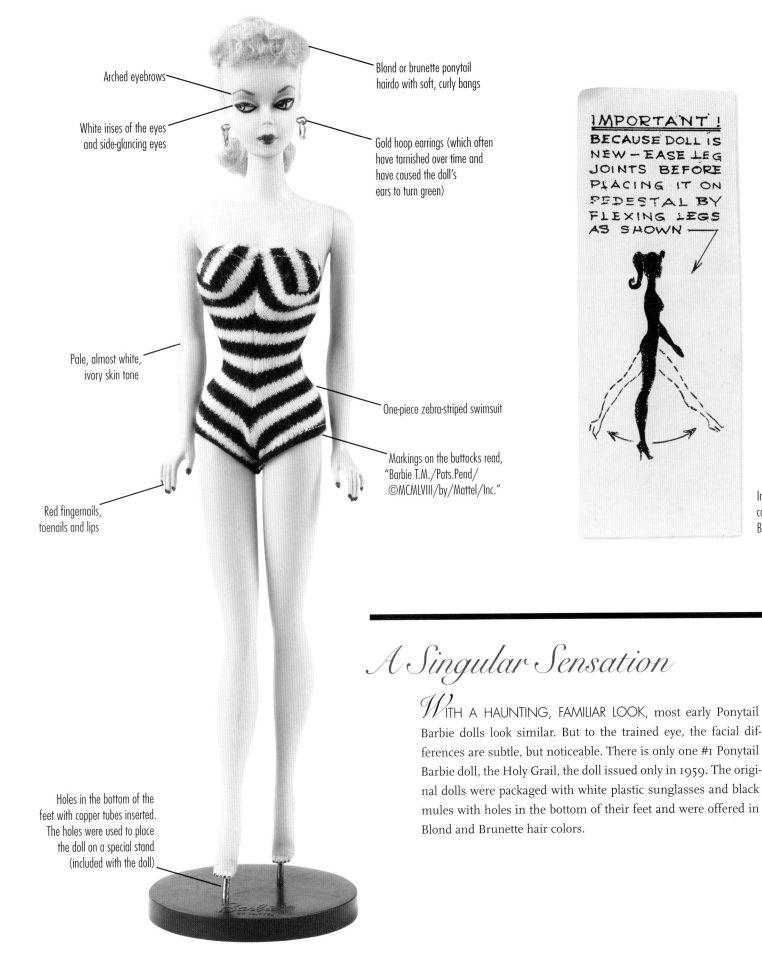

Arched eyebrows

White irises of the eyes
and side-glancing eyes

Blond or brunette ponytail
hairdo with soft, curly bangs

Gold hoop earrings (which often
have tarnished over time and
have caused the doll's
ears to turn green)

Pale, almost white,
ivory skin tone

One-piece zebra-striped swimsuit

Red fingernails,
toenails and lips

Markings on the buttocks read,
"Barbie T.M./Pats.Pend/
©MCMLVIII/by/Mattel/Inc."

Holes in the bottom of the
feet with copper tubes inserted.
The holes were used to place
the doll on a special stand
(included with the doll)

IMPORTANT!
BECAUSE DOLL IS
NEW — EASE LEG
JOINTS BEFORE
PLACING IT ON
PEDESTAL BY
FLEXING LEGS
AS SHOWN →

Instructions that
came with a #1
Barbie doll.

A Singular Sensation

WITH A HAUNTING, FAMILIAR LOOK, most early Ponytail
Barbie dolls look similar. But to the trained eye, the facial differences are subtle, but noticeable. There is only one #1 Ponytail
Barbie doll, the Holy Grail, the doll issued only in 1959. The original dolls were packaged with white plastic sunglasses and black
mules with holes in the bottom of their feet and were offered in
Blond and Brunette hair colors.

Available only in select stores to highlight new Barbie dolls and her outfits, this special Pink Silhouette Dressed Box #1 Blond Ponytail Barbie doll remains in phenomenal condition more than 50 years after her release. Barbie wears a Winter Holiday outfit (#975). The original outfit included pull-on stretch pants (with feet) and back zipper, a knit hooded T-shirt with back zipper and a fabric cord ties under her chin, and a white leather-like car coat with red fleecy lining. Finishing touches included cork wedgies with white uppers and red vinyl gloves. A red plaid vinyl zippered bag was also included.

The Grand Plan

*R*UTH HANDLER WANTED LITTLE GIRLS TO DREAM their own dreams. That's why she envisioned Barbie doll without a predetermined or fixed personality. Instead, Handler wanted children to develop their own perception of the doll. Fittingly, Ponytail Barbie doll came with little more than a black and white zebra-striped swimsuit. Although a wide range of outfits and careers would be offered, the final decisions on career path and fashion statement would be up to children.

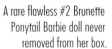

A rare flawless #2 Brunette Ponytail Barbie doll never removed from her box.

#1 Brunette Ponytail Barbie doll.

#1 Blond Ponytail Barbie doll.

*H*ERE YOU CAN SEE the subtle changes to Barbie's face from #1 through #5 Ponytail.

#1 Ponytail Barbie doll (#850), clad in a now-famous black-and-white one-piece swimsuit, was only available for one year before Mattel made subtle changes to her look. Both blonds and brunettes were made; the harder-to-find brunette remains more desirable — and costly — to collectors.

#2 Ponytail Barbie doll, also issued in 1959, was almost identical to #1. The difference: she does not have holes in her feet, allowing for a slightly different stand.

Issued in 1960, #3 Ponytail Barbie doll offered a softer face with muted makeup, blue eyes and gently curved eyebrows.

#4 Ponytail Barbie doll was also issued in 1960 with a new, improved vinyl that retained its color. She also wears only blue eyeliner.

Barbie ™

In 1961, #5 Ponytail Barbie doll was made of hollow plastic. She was also offered with vivid Red hair referred to as Titian, and also as a Brunette. She was the first doll to wear a wrist band.

A new decade brought
new style and excitement
to Barbie doll's world,
including the Let's Dance
and Swingin' Easy
outfits shown here.

34

CHAPTER 2

The 1960s

Barbie Welcomes Change in Style

*Y*OUTH DOMINATED THE CULTURE of the 1960s. And you can credit World War II for that. The postwar Baby Boom resulted in 70 million teenagers coming of age in the decade. It was youth that shaped the fashion, the fads and the politics of the decade. And all of that shaped Barbie.

Both inside and outside the world of Barbie, change was definitely the theme of the 1960s. If the previous decade was defined by the hula hoop, Elvis and a certain Father-Knows-Best simplicity, the '60s were marked by the promise of JFK in the White House, the advancement of the Civil Rights Movement and the magic and mud of three days of peace and music at Woodstock. The decade that started with Alan Shepard as the first American in space in 1961 ended with Neil Armstrong as the first man to walk on the moon in 1969. In between it all, the only constant seemed to be change.

The same was true of Barbie, who had evolved into one of the hottest-selling toys of all time at the beginning of the decade. Consider that in the first few years of the decade, Barbie assembled an inspired wardrobe, a boyfriend, a car and her very own Dream Home. No wonder this fashion model go-getter had her own fan club.

Bubblecuts Begin, 1961

*A*FTER ENDURING all the facelifts of 1959 and 1960, Barbie doll adopted somewhat of a standard look—but not for long. Once her look had mellowed in the Ponytail age, Barbie shook the toy world with one simple move: she cut her hair.

In 1961, Barbie doll, although still delightfully perky in her ponytail, was given an alternate hairdo—a shorter, bouffant cut called the Bubblecut (dolls with ponytail hairdos, however, were still available until 1966).

Bubblecuts represent the first major hairstyle change for Barbie doll, an element that would be key to the doll's development over the next 50 years. The doll's chameleon attributes have often been connected to her coiffure.

By the Bubblecut era, Barbie doll had traded in her black-and-white swimsuit for a plain red one-piece, and the hairstyle was offered in a variety of colors—blond, titian (a reddish blond), brunette, brownette (deep brown) and variations—as well as styles (the side-part Bubblecut, with the hair combed to one side, is a valuable variation for collectors).

Bubblecut Barbie doll in original red swimsuit.

A bevy of Bubblecut Barbie dolls in Best Bow dress variations.

Pretty in Pink

*R*ELEASED IN 1964, the spectacular Sparkling Pink Gift Set is a coveted item for any Barbie doll collector. The set came with a Bubblecut Barbie doll featuring full, bright, cotton candy pink lips. Included with the doll was a pink sparkle ensemble that featured a hat, bolero jacket, bolero one-shoulder top, a short wrap skirt, knee length coat and silver glittered heels. Doll came dressed in a pink helenca swimsuit. Mattel released a vintage reproduction of the set in 2009.

This Bubblecut Barbie doll features the rare white ginger hair color.

𝒯HIS BLOND BUBBLECUT Barbie doll made
the transition from the work world to social life
look easy in the stylish basic black dress fashion
outfit, After Five. Introduced in 1962, After Five
featured a big, white picture hat that framed
Barbie's face with flattering softness and also
black open toe heels.

THE HAIR APPARENT
Fashion Queen, 1963

SHE WASN'T QUITE CLEOPATRA, but Fashion Queen's turban certainly created such an allure.

Dressed in a shiny gold and white striped swimsuit, Fashion Queen wore a matching turban to cover her molded hair, which was a first for the doll. Wigs included with the set allowed Fashion Queen to transform her hair from blond bubblecut to red flip to brunette pageboy.

Plenty of little boys may have pulled the heads off their sisters' Barbie dolls. But the Fashion Queen Wig Wardrobe set may have inspired some girls to try that themselves. Sold separately from the doll, the Wig Wardrobe included three wigs and just the head of Fashion Queen. This allowed kids to mix and match dolls, heads and hairstyles.

Fashion Queen Barbie doll.

FASHION QUEEN was the first Barbie doll without rooted hair. Instead, this innovative Barbie used wigs to change her appearance.

Swirl Ponytail, 1964

*E*VEN THOUGH THE 1960S heralded a decade of new hairstyles for Barbie doll, the ponytail didn't simply vanish. In 1964, Mattel introduced the stylish and elegant new Swirl Ponytail hairstyle. The soft bangs found on earlier Ponytails were replaced with a soft upsweep of hair. Variations were endless; dolls have been found with Ash Blond, Platinum, Lemon Blond, Brunette and Titian color hair; lip color also varied widely, from red and coral to white and almost lavender.

The doll's elegance was unparalleled for its time. Not only was the hairstyle more chic than previous styles, a new wave of eye-catching colors for hair and lips added interest and impact.

This stunning Platinum Swirl Barbie doll models an equally rare Japanese version of Garden Tea Party fashion outfit from 1964. This red paisley version of the outfit was made from the same pattern used for 1962's Garden Party (#931). The accessories include short white gloves and white open-toe heels.

Miss Barbie, 1964

Pretty in pink, Miss Barbie doll could hit the beach in three distinct wigs.

*M*OLDED HAIR, previously seen on Fashion Queen, reappeared on Miss Barbie—one of the more innovative Barbie dolls of the decade.

There's a reason this unusual-looking doll had a faraway glance . . . this doll was the first (and last) Barbie doll to have "sleep eyes" that opened and closed. Because of this, her head was hard plastic, rather than soft vinyl. Designed as a beach beauty in pink glittery swimsuit and cap, Miss Barbie could hardly romp on the sand without another innovation—bendable legs.

Without her shower cap, the molded-hair Miss Barbie could get wigged out, just like her predecessor, Fashion Queen.

American Girl, 1965

MATURITY. RESPECT. BENDABLE LEGS. You could say that by 1965, Barbie doll grew up and came into her own with the comfortable American Girl look. The only innovation to stay from the previous year was bendable legs, which would become a standard for most of the Barbie dolls to follow. Mattel referred to this doll as simply Bendable Leg Barbie. Due to its hairstyle, however, it has come to be universally known as the American Girl.

American Girls featured more tailored, bobbed hair with straight bangs. Rarer variations featured a side-part hairdo. The doll's swimsuit had evolved from a staid solid-color one-piece into a more stylish multi-stripe top with turquoise bottom; box art had also evolved. Boxes now featured a full-length image of the doll, focusing on the bendable leg feature.

It's easy to see why American Girl Barbie doll was chosen Campus Sweetheart at the Valentine's Day dance. Dazzlingly in this 1965 outfit (#1616), Barbie received a bouquet of six red satin roses with "ferns" of green feathers. She was awarded a silver-colored metal loving cup with a raised "B."

CAMPUS HERO
(without doll) #770
Campus leader Ken proudly wears the handsome sweater Barbie knit for him adds white duck pants, red socks and white oxfords. Taking Barbie to the big pre-game rally and dance, he shows his University letter, leads the crowd's cheers with his banner The set. $3.00

Brio Store Display
American Girl in Campus Sweetheart

THIS ITEM CERTAINLY WILL GO down as one of the rarest vintage Barbie doll items that has been ever been consigned to auction. Brio, who was a distributor for Mattel in Scandinavia in the 1960s, distributed custom store displays and dressed box dolls which rarely surface. Brio had a company policy that required dealers to return all promotional merchandise back to Brio. As a result these special items normally have not survived for collectors to acquire. This incredible item features Swedish graphics on a beautifully preserved display board, and also showcases an amazing long haired American Girl dressed in a mint and complete "Campus Sweetheart" outfit. What is intriguing about this piece is that the graphics relate to the 1965 version of Barbie's Queen of the Prom Game, and feature the white box illustration of this game. Research indicates that this may have been a store display relating to the introduction of the Queen of the Prom Game, as the Swedish writing on the display refers to "Barbie Playing Queen of the Ball."

This doll is an amazing long hair brunette, with deep coral lips, striking face paint and dark brows. Original cello on head, hair is pristine. She came attached to the display board. She is wearing a pristine and complete Campus Sweetheart, her red open-toe heels are pinned to her feet through her soles and she holds her shiny silver loving cup in her left hand, roses are in her right hand. The loving cup and roses have been sewn on to her gloves. We do recognize that Campus Sweetheart, US Version, came with pink heels, and feel that the red heels were original to the Scandinavian market. The display board is a two layered fiberboard construction, the underlying board is bright yellow. The top layer is painted black and has red, white and yellow graphics. This doll sold for $8,400 in Doll Attic's auction.

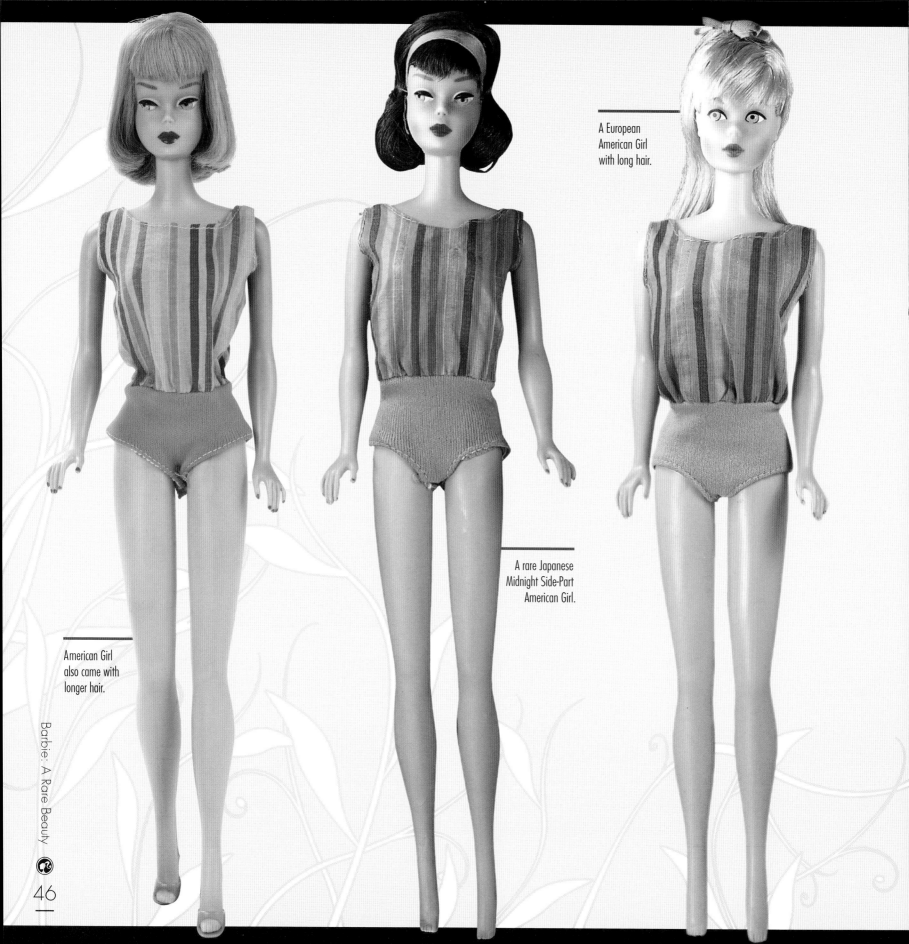

A European
American Girl
with long hair.

A rare Japanese
Midnight Side-Part
American Girl.

American Girl
also came with
longer hair.

Color Magic, 1966

*F*UTURE ALCHEMISTS AND HAIRDRESSERS could have learned their trades with this creative doll. If it wasn't enough for girls to dress and accessorize their dolls, now they could dye their dolls' hair. The innovative color-changing solution was mild, yet effective enough to create magical effects.

Two long-haired versions (with side-part hair) were available; Golden Blond hair could change to Scarlet Flame (and back again) and Midnight could change to Ruby Red. The doll's diamond print swimsuit would also change colors when swabbed with the solution. There was also a sampling of Platinums made which were never mass produced. In testing the Platinum hair color Mattel determined it ws too difficult to change the hair color. True Platinums are thought to be factory samples, bearing a slender face.

Three Color Magic beauties illustrate the hair color variations.

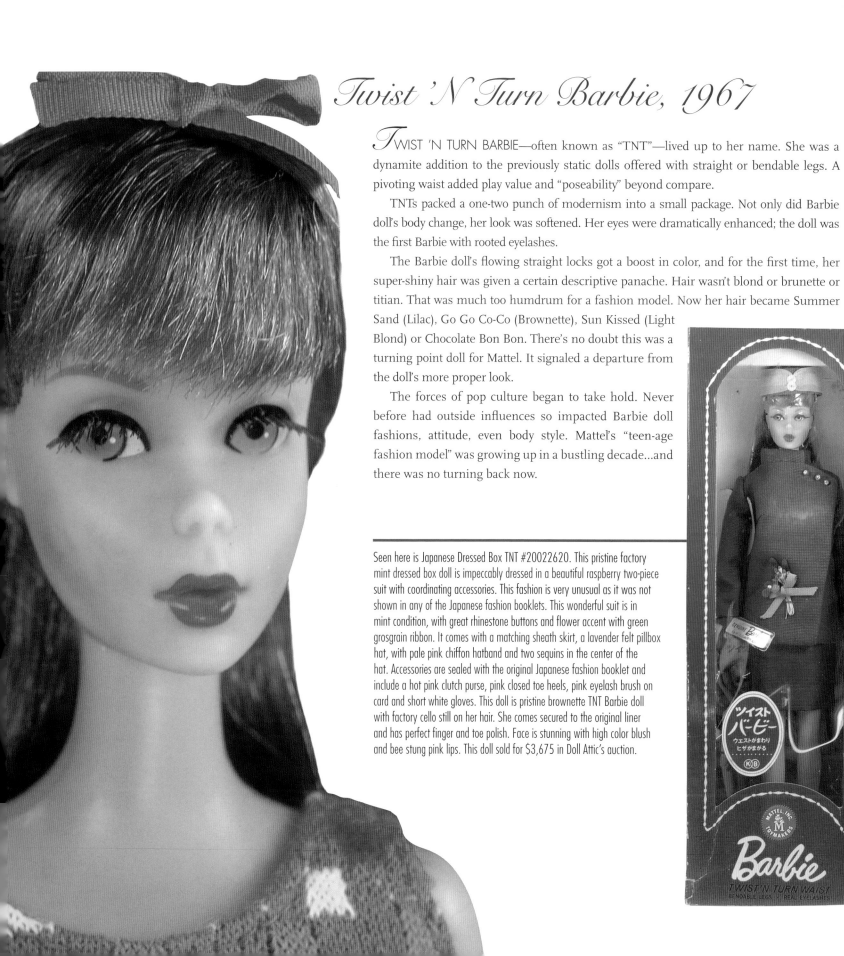

Twist 'N Turn Barbie, 1967

TWIST 'N TURN BARBIE—often known as "TNT"—lived up to her name. She was a dynamite addition to the previously static dolls offered with straight or bendable legs. A pivoting waist added play value and "poseability" beyond compare.

TNTs packed a one-two punch of modernism into a small package. Not only did Barbie doll's body change, her look was softened. Her eyes were dramatically enhanced; the doll was the first Barbie with rooted eyelashes.

The Barbie doll's flowing straight locks got a boost in color, and for the first time, her super-shiny hair was given a certain descriptive panache. Hair wasn't blond or brunette or titian. That was much too humdrum for a fashion model. Now her hair became Summer Sand (Lilac), Go Go Co-Co (Brownette), Sun Kissed (Light Blond) or Chocolate Bon Bon. There's no doubt this was a turning point doll for Mattel. It signaled a departure from the doll's more proper look.

The forces of pop culture began to take hold. Never before had outside influences so impacted Barbie doll fashions, attitude, even body style. Mattel's "teen-age fashion model" was growing up in a bustling decade...and there was no turning back now.

Seen here is Japanese Dressed Box TNT #20022620. This pristine factory mint dressed box doll is impeccably dressed in a beautiful raspberry two-piece suit with coordinating accessories. This fashion is very unusual as it was not shown in any of the Japanese fashion booklets. This wonderful suit is in mint condition, with great rhinestone buttons and flower accent with green grosgrain ribbon. It comes with a matching sheath skirt, a lavender felt pillbox hat, with pale pink chiffon hatband and two sequins in the center of the hat. Accessories are sealed with the original Japanese fashion booklet and include a hot pink clutch purse, pink closed toe heels, pink eyelash brush on card and short white gloves. This doll is pristine brownette TNT Barbie doll with factory cello still on her hair. She comes secured to the original liner and has perfect finger and toe polish. Face is stunning with high color blush and bee stung pink lips. This doll sold for $3,675 in Doll Attic's auction.

Talking Barbie, 1968

$\mathscr{F}$OR NINE YEARS, BARBIE DOLLS had been silent—remember, they were vessels in which little girls could channel their emotions, thoughts and speech. But the late 1960s gave birth to a new technology that Mattel was using in other toys—a talking mechanism.

Not exactly a Chatty Cathy, Talking Barbie (with the mod TNT body and a pull-string on her back) talked about fashion, dates, the prom, shopping and parties.

To expand Barbie doll's audience, Mattel also marketed Talking Barbie doll in a Spanish-speaking version. As the years passed, Barbie dolls were released that could speak many languages, including French, German, Dutch and Italian.

The Talking Barbie doll had something to say while wearing Pink Premiere Gift Set fashion. The white varitation of the outfit is a sample and the only one known to exist.

Mane Attraction

Special Issue Carnation Ponytail with factory side-swept ponytail.

$\mathcal{N}$OT ALL PONYTAIL BARBIE DOLLS are created equal. The doll's face and body style, of course, subtly evolved through the years. Often overlooked, however, are the many different ponytail variations of the doll. Here are pristine examples of those variations—many thought not to exist until they were discovered.

#1 Brunette with original hard curl in ponytail.

#2 Blond with original bands in hair.

#5 Brunette with factory hair curl.

Blond Swirl Ponytail with double row wrap in hair.

#4 Brunette in factory bun.

#4 Blond Ponytail with factory braided elaborate ponytail.

#3 Ponytail Dressed Box doll with factory up-do in hair.

Barbie doll and Ken
doll were hip to moving
on down the road as
the Seventies arrived.

CHAPTER 3

The 1970s

Barbie Makes Her Moves

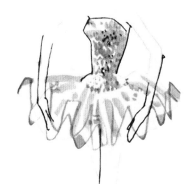

*I*T SEEMED THE ENTIRE COUNTRY was on the move in the 1970s. The Seventies was a decade of action—some fascinating, some comical, and some simply odd. The Beatles moved on, releasing their last album in 1970. Nike hit the ground running. Motorcycle daredevil Evel Knievel jumped the Snake River Canyon, sort of. Nixon resigned. Oil prices jumped. Comet Kohoutek fizzled. Jimmy Hoffa disappeared. The Vietnam War ended. Apple Computer began. Bicentennial celebrations rocked the U.S. Disco dominated. Women's skirts went short. Hair went long.

Who could keep up?

In an era of action, Barbie doll was no exception. More than anything, Mattel strove to bring Barbie and her friends to life. The company opened the decade with its most ambitious doll to date—Dramatic New Living Barbie, which was fully poseable from head to foot. In 1972, Mattel released Walk Lively Barbie, a doll who could walk by herself; Busy Barbie, a doll who could hold things in her poseable hands; and Busy Talking Barbie, a talking version of Busy Barbie.

Moving bodies, growing hair and a kissing mechanism were some additional actions Mattel dreamed up for the dolls for the 1970s.

Of course, the decade wasn't only about movement. Malibu Barbie, a sun-tanned goddess with straight blond hair and painted eyelashes, was an instant hit. Superstar Barbie was released at the height of the disco craze. In a feel-good era of style and sound, Superstar Barbie was decidedly different from the traditional visages of the doll's early years.

Dramatic New Changes

A VERITABLE EARTHQUAKE OF ACTIVITY shook up the Barbie dolls Mattel introduced at the turn of the decade. Dramatic New Living Barbie doll arrived in 1970, and if you didn't notice her futuristic silver and gold lamé swimsuit, you couldn't miss the doll's new attitude.

While Twist 'n Turn was an important innovation for its time, it was elementary compared to the range of motion of Dramatic New Living Barbie doll. TNT could twist, but this doll could move.

Fully poseable, Dramatic New Living Barbie doll featured vivid face paint, rooted eyelashes, bendable legs, twisting waist (for all those shimmies and shakes), bendable elbows and wrists (to strike those disco poses), a rotating head and loose leg and arm sockets (wanna see her do the splits?). This lifelike doll could sit, bend and strike many other flexible poses.

By 1971, however, it wasn't enough that Barbie doll could twist, turn, bend her legs, swivel and move her hips. Now she could walk.

Even though Walk Lively Barbie doll wore pilgrim heels, not white go-go boots, she could walk smoothly (and swing her arms accordingly) on a special stand.

Dramatic New Living Barbie doll, 1970.

Walk Lively Barbie doll, 1971.

The groovy gauchos set epitomized the mod look of the 1970s.

Francie Wild 'n Wooly outfit.

GOING MOBILE
Live Action Barbie, 1970

*W*ITH THE AGE OF AQUARIUS DAWNING, Barbie doll needed to be ready in a psychedelic swirled get-up, adorned with faux suede fringe. Hippie chic had arrived and was reflected in Barbie doll attitude, body, hair and fashions.

The 1970s were definitely in full swing, at least where this doll was concerned. Like her Dramatic New Living counterpart, Live Action Barbie doll was movin' and groovin'. Thanks to a special stand, Live Action Barbie doll could "dance to your favorite music." One touch of the "touch and go" stand set off a whirling dervish of frantic dancing. Live Action Barbie doll's box touted her moves—"I dance to your favorite music," "I dance more than ever before," "Start the action, touch my touch n' go stand," and "There's lots I do—just like you."

Barbie doll's friends Ken, Christie and P.J. also got in on the fun, with Live Action variations—all dressed in wickedly authentic 1970s fashions.

Left to right: Talking Busy Steffie, Busy Steffie, Busy Ken, Busy Barbie, Busy Francie and Talking Busy Barbie.

THE TALKING VERSION OF BUSY BARBIE
SAID THE FOLLOWING PHRASES:

"I think I'll call Ken."
"Why don't you come over for dinner?"
"Let's put on some music."
"There's a new rock show on TV."
"I'm making a new party dress."
"Help me fix my hair."

Let's Get Busy

RELEASED IN 1971, BUSY BARBIE featured delicate "working" hands. The mechanical looking "gripping" hands allowed Barbie doll to "hold" accessories, such as a groovy record player. Far out!

While the innovations on this doll were designed to make Barbie doll more active and powerful ("gripping" hands, TNT waist), they ultimately didn't last long. Production costs were prohibitive, and the dolls' joints a bit too fragile to survive a lot of play.

Busy Barbie, like the other motion-packed dolls before her, was awash in a sea of gimmicks Mattel had implemented during this time. And like Live Action Barbie doll, the "busy" feature was soon incorporated into Ken, Francie and other Barbie doll friends.

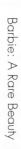

The Long and Short of It

During the decade, baby dolls were eclipsed by the popularity of fashion dolls. Why? Little girls loved the hair play possible with fashion dolls. It quickly became a craze embraced by many doll makers of the day.

Released in 1970, Barbie with Growin' Pretty Hair (#1144) featured tresses that could be lengthened or shortened with a mild tug. Barbie doll's retractable ponytail embraced the hair play craze; she even came with hairpieces and accessories to complete the look.

Young aspiring hairstylists loved this doll; it offered hours of practice and dozens of hair-style possibilities. But one swift snip of the scissors often left the Barbie doll in need of a real stylist to fix the damage.

A department store exclusive, Barbie Hair Happenin's came with center-parted, short titian hair, real rooted eyelashes, and a Twist 'N Turn body. Her outfit featured a white blouson top and pink skirt. What really set Barbie Hair Happenin's apart, however, was the three titian wigs: mini curls, midi swirls and fashion fall. The doll is considered by collectors as one of the beautiful and desired dolls of the mod-era.

Barbie with Growin' Pretty Hair allowed little girls to change the length of the doll's hair.

This Hair Happenin's Barbie doll from 1971 sold for $1,250 at a 2006 auction.

Malibu Barbie, 1971

$\mathcal{B}$ARBIE LOOKED LIKE A NATIVE CALIFORNIA GIRL with her blissfully tanned skin, her blue-eyed blond hair surfer girl look (even though her roots peg her to be a native of Willows, Wisconsin). Malibu Barbie was one of the earliest dolls to hit the essence of little girls' play patterns. Sure, hair play was hot, but taking Barbie doll to the beach or the pool was just plain cool. The look made such a splash that just about every Barbie doll friend was soon "Malibu-ized." It also spawned a number of licensed products, such as paper dolls and coloring books.

Malibu
Barbie doll.

Malibu Barbie
doll reproduction.

Montgomery Ward Barbie, 1972

*I*N ONE OF THE FIRST REISSUES OF BARBIE DOLL, Mattel in 1972 created a reproduction of an early brunette Ponytail Barbie (#3210) to commemorate the 100th anniversary of Montgomery Ward stores. Dressed in the familiar black-and-white swimsuit, the doll was sold in stores in a sparsely illustrated pink box under the name "The Original Barbie." Dolls ordered through the stores catalog were shipped in plain boxes.

The doll was notable because the age of reproductions and store exclusives had begun—something that would continue throughout Barbie doll's history.

Montgomery Ward Malibu Barbie exclusive.

The 1972 Montgomery Ward's Barbie doll was the first reissue of sorts for Mattel.

Quick Curl Barbie, 1973

$\mathcal{B}$ASIC HAIR PLAY TOOK ON AN ADDED DIMENSION with Quick Curl Barbie doll. This very demure doll featured hair that really curled and straightened with the help of a special plastic curling wand, comb and brush. Whether you were an aspiring hairdresser or simply liked to play with hair, Quick Curl Barbie doll was there for any hair-brained fun you might want.

Quick Curl Barbie doll capitalized on the popularity of hair play in the 1970s.

Quick Curl PJ.

Here She is, Miss America

*N*ATURALLY, IF YOU START OUT AS A TEENAGE FASHION MODEL you just might aspire one day to be Miss America. And with quick curl hair on your side, why not dream big? In 1974 Barbie doll fulfilled many a little girl's fantasy when we was crowned Quick Curl Miss America (#8697) of the doll world.

Superstar Barbie, 1977

*R*IGHT IN STEP WITH THE DISCO BALLS AND FLASHY CLOTHES
of the late 1970s was Superstar Barbie doll—a glitzy addition to the decade.

After almost 20 years and dozens of reincarnations, this Barbie doll had
a decidedly different face from the stoic visages of Barbie doll's early years.
Glamour was the watchword, and Barbie doll's new wide blue eyes and smil-
ing face would become a long-term look for the doll.

Supersize Barbie, 1977

*T*HERE'S A REASON MOST BARBIE DOLLS—
then and now—remain just 11-1/2 inches tall.
When you've got it right, you don't mess with
success. Mattel learned that lesson with
Supersize Barbie doll. It was the experiment
that just never caught on.

It's uncertain what the mo-
tivation was to turn Barbie
doll into an Amazon (at 18
inches, she towered over
the other dolls). Trouble was,
Supersize Barbie couldn't
share her friends' clothes,
didn't fit into their houses and
wouldn't feel comfortable
at a slumber party.

Includes
Wear 'n Share™ jewelry.
Crown, necklace,
earrings and ring
for Barbie;
necklace, ring and
barrette for you!

SuperSize
Barbie

...nge her looks in so many ways!
...ensemble! Glittery jewelry!
...streaked hair!

MATTEL

Black Barbie doll.

CHAPTER 4

The 1980s
Barbie Takes a World View

$\mathcal{T}$HE EIGHTIES GAVE US tight stonewashed jeans, scrunch socks and spandex—lots of spandex. It also introduced Madonna, Miami Vice, Reagan in the White House and the shocking news that Darth Vader was Luke's father.

Of course, we also witnessed the world-changing collapse of the Berlin Wall. With the wall coming down, the world quickly became a much smaller place.

While Mattel may have introduced Barbie to America in 1959, in the 1980s Barbie doll introduced the world to little girls. The globetrotting Barbie doll broke free and crossed barriers previously untested. She would become a citizen of the world through the International Series (now called Dolls of the World), which effortlessly transported Barbie doll (and, vicariously, the little girls who played with her) to far-flung places some children and adults could only dream about visiting: Italy, Spain, Ireland, Paris, Nigeria, Kenya, Russia, Iceland, Malaysia, Japan and many others were among the exotic locales Barbie called home. Her fashions and accessories relayed the customs and culture of other lands, helping to make the world a little bit smaller—and a lot more fashionable—for children of all ages.

Black Francie,
Barbie doll's cousin,
was first introduced
in the late 1960s.

Black Barbie doll.

Black Barbie, 1980

MATTEL FORAYED INTO THE MULTICULTURAL domain about a decade before the introduction of Black Barbie doll with the introduction of Black Francie, Barbie doll's cousin. Barbie doll's African-American friend, Christie, also appeared in the late 1960s.

But Barbie doll herself wasn't given the ethnic edge until 1980s. Based on the Twist 'N Turn doll, Black Barbie doll was described on her box as "black, beautiful and dynamite." She featured a bold, stylish red gown with gold accents and tailored afro hair. This was a watershed moment for Mattel. In embracing other cultures, Mattel firmly established Barbie as a doll for every girl. For the rest of her history, the doll has been available in Caucasian and African-American versions, as well as other ethnicities.

Hispanic Barbie, 1980

¿QUÉ PASA, BARBIE? It turns out that quite a bit was happening in Barbie doll's world. To meet the demands of a growing ethnic market, Mattel released its first Hispanic Barbie doll. Hispanic Barbie doll (#1292) was released primarily in Spanish-speaking markets. With the changes in dress and face molds seen on these ethnic dolls, Mattel was paving the way for its forthcoming International Series.

International Series/Dolls of the World, 1980-present

MATTEL'S SECOND SERIES AIMED DIRECTLY AT ADULT COLLECTORS TOOK AIM AT THE WORLD—and truly skyrocketed Barbie doll to a global phenomenon. Barbie became a citizen of the globe through the International Series, which effortlessly transported Barbie doll (and, vicariously, the little girls who played with her) to far-flung places some children and adults could only dream about visiting. The dolls' fashions and accessories relayed the customs and culture of other lands, helping embrace other ethnicities.

Cheerio! Ciao! Bonjour! Europe was first on Barbie doll's ticket to ride—the first three countries Barbie doll would pay tribute to were England, Italy and France. While many children and adults already considered Barbie doll a queen, the first doll in the series, Royal Barbie, featured Barbie doll as a British royal. With tiara and sash, she could have been mistaken as a Miss America contestant. Italian Barbie, dressed in peasant blouse, featured a unique head mold. And ooh la la, Parisian Barbie (which utilized the Steffie head mold) was the stereotypical can-can dancer. Several of the earlier dolls were reissued with new faces and attire, and after a few years, Mattel renamed the line "Dolls of the World." The series, truly history personified, has targeted all corners of the globe; all seven continents have been represented.

Released in 2005 as part of the Dolls of the World Series, Princess of the Pacific Islands Barbie doll wears a traditional island dress and a lei.

In tribute to Rio de Janeiro's joyous, week-long celebration, Carnaval Barbie doll (2006) wears a Brazilian costume featuring a bright purple outfit with a halter top and a short skirt.

Chinese New Year begins with the new moon on the first day of the year and ends with the full moon 15 days later. This ancient Asian festival finds Chinese New Year Barbie doll (2006) wearing a red dress featuring traditional Chinese motifs.

Western Barbie, 1980

CAPITALIZING ON THE COWBOY CRAZE of the new decade fueled by John Travolta's "Urban Cowboy," Mattel released Western Barbie (#1757). Not only did Western Barbie doll come complete in cowgirl fashion, she featured something unique: a winking eye. Although the feature may have put a little giddy-up in Ken's step the winking feature never caught on and was not used in future models. Joining Barbie on the range were Western Skipper

Dream Date Barbie, 1983

YOU CAN EASILY PICTURE DREAM DATE BARBIE (#5868) hailing a cab as easily as waving from the window of her limo. And why not? This go-getter epitomized Barbie doll's 1980s look with doe eyes, a Superstar face and cascades of blond hair—that was the fresh, healthy glow the 1980s dolls sported. And the word in 1980s fashion was "excess." With a sequined top, satin skirt and twinkly earrings, this Barbie doll was, indeed, a dream date.

Dream Date Barbie doll was just one of many similar-looking blue-eyed, blond haired 1980s dolls. Painted faces and clothes may have changed, but underneath it all, the Superstar mold and TNT body remained a standard for more than 10 years.

Happy Holidays Series, 1988-1998

SINCE BARBIE DOLL'S INCEPTION, MATTEL had sold countless number of Barbie dolls to adults—but the dolls ultimately were purchased for children. But by 1988, Mattel had come to the realization that adults might also be the end user of the dolls—and that opened up an entirely new market for Barbie. The Happy Holidays series marked the beginning of a "collector series," intended for adults to buy, display and collect. And that meant that the dolls could likely be sold for a higher price point.

Still, based on the other dolls on the market, it was unthinkable—possibly even to Mattel—that anyone would pay more than $10 for a Barbie doll. But the high-quality Happy Holidays doll and packaging raised the price to $19.99. The good news was that the doll was an instant success, surpassing perhaps even Mattel's wildest dreams.

Until this time, Mattel had been satisfying consumer demand—making dolls little girls would play with. But Mattel learned an important collecting lesson with this series—the the fine line between satisfying consumer demand and satisfying collector demand.

Consumers want dolls to be readily available. Collectors, however, covet limited production numbers; too much supply can dash the doll's collector value.

High demand (and short supply) for the first Happy Holidays doll caused Mattel to steadily increase the number of dolls produced each year. Eventually, a glut occurred, leaving dazzling dolls languishing on store shelves long after the holiday season.

Low production numbers and high demand are directly responsible for the first Happy Holidays doll's high secondary market value. Later issues are worth considerably less.

Happy Holidays was not originally intended as a continuing series, but it became one of the longest lasting and most successful Barbie doll series, lasting until 1998.

It directly influenced the era of higher-end collectible dolls, opening the door to dolls that soared past the retail price ceiling. Due to the acceptance of Happy Holidays, consumers seemed ready to embrace higher prices for higher-quality collectible dolls.

Happy Holidays Barbie doll #1, 1988.

1989

The second in the Happy Holiday Series, Barbie looked like a winter princess. Dressed in a white gown trimmed with faux fur, white glitter tulle and satin skirt and faux fur stile, Barbie doll put the wonder in Winter Wonderland.

1990

A White or African American version of Happy Holidays #3 was offered. Both versions wore a fuchsia and silver gown.

1991

Happy Holidays #4 wore a long sleeve, sweetheart neck, full skirted, green velvet gown with silver, red, and green sequin trim on the bodice. Barbie doll also came with a matching evening bag and silver and red bead drop earrings.

1992

Stunning in her long sleeve silver gown with white tulle and silver glitter accents, beaded sequined bodice and sleeves, Happy Holidays #5 put the glamour in any holiday ball.

1993

Similar to the first in the series, the sixth Happy Holidays Barbie doll in 1993 was a radiant lady in red. Her gown featured a golden bodice, red tulle with golden glitter and a golden edged skirt. Poinsettias adorned the bodice while red satin bows on the shoulders completed the sensational seasonal look.

1994

Barbie made even the harshest winter warm with this stunning Happy Holidays #7 offering. With her faux fur and long sleeve, sweetheart neck, gold lame gown, Barbie doll took the chill out of any evening.

1995

In a festive green holly-printed dress with a silvery Victorian collar, Barbie personified the charm of the season. Her ensemble in Happy Holidays #8 was accented by red rhinestone berries, a poinsettia sash and a jeweled choker.

1996

In a charming burgundy velvet coat trimmed in luxurious white faux fur, Barbie doll welcomes the holiday season. Underneath her lovely velvet coat is a golden-tiered skirt. A gorgeous white faux fur muff and hat match the fur accents at her collar and sleeves.

1998

The 1998 Happy Holidays Barbie doll is sophisticated and elegant in a holiday theme gown in rich black velvety fabric with exquisite silver glitter accents. This was the only offering in the series to come in black. A pink cape and jeweled tiara accent this stunning ensemble. As a bonus, this doll carries the distinction of the being the first in the Happy Holidays series to wear her hair styled in an elegant upsweep.

1997

In Happy Holidays #10 released in 1997, Barbie doll is a true image of royal splendor in holiday red, snowy white and glittering gold with a golden tiara adorned with six ruby-colored gemstones. Festive accents include a jeweled choker and earrings.

Change her lip color with water!

Released in 1989, Dance Magic Barbie doll featured a change-around dress that allowed Barbie to go from dancing at a formal affair, then change into a ballerina, and finally hit the disco. And that's not all! Cold water applied to Barbie's lips allowed you to turn them red. Applying warm water turned her lips back to pink.

Dance Magic Barbie

New from Barbie

Great Shape Barbie WORKOUT CENTER

How does Barbie doll stay so fit? It's easy with the Great Shape Barbie Workout Center, advertised her in a rare store display. Great Shape Barbie doll was released in 1983 in leotard, leg warmers, colorful sash, sweatband, bag and exercise book.

We girls can do anything... right, Barbie!

Barbie doll booklets from the 1980s illustrate the spirit and glitz of the era.

My First Barbie, part of the pink box line, debuted in 1983. The author gave this doll to her daughter, Jessica, in 1983 — the year she was born.

FOR AGES OVER 3.

DEAR MOM – My First BARBIE® has
• smooth straight legs for easy dressing
• mix 'n match outfit

Dear Jessica; This doll was bought the year you were born. treasure it. Keep it for your own children to enjoy. Always Love mommy 3-28-83

My First Barbie®

Easy-to-dress doll for the younger child

No. 1875

SAFETY TESTED Conforms to PS 72-76

MATTEL

Serenade in Satin Barbie doll from 1997's Couture Collection is an exquisite example of creating dolls for the adult collector, a trend that evolved rapidly in the 1990s.

SERENADE IN SATIN.
Barbie DOLL

CHAPTER 5

The 1990s
Barbie Evolves into Collector Icon

*T*HE NINETIES GAVE US SUCH FILM CLASSICS AS *APOLLO 13, Braveheart, Saving Private Ryan, Titanic* and *Pulp Fiction*. The decade also gave us two classic animated films aimed at children: *Beauty and the Beast* and *Toy Story*. The funny thing about those two movies is adults enjoyed them as much as children.

The same phenomenon occurred with Barbie doll.

By the 1990s, little girls were not the only viable market for Barbie dolls. Adult collectors were making up an increasingly larger audience, one that was willing to pay top dollar for higher-quality dolls.

Of paramount import to collectors was quality and edition size. The Bob Mackie series, especially, is an example of how higher-end dolls (often retailing for $100 or more) have thrived in a collector climate, both on the retail and secondary markets.

The era of Barbie doll as collectible had begun in a big way; no longer was there concern that collectors wouldn't pay premium prices for a well-executed, limited-edition Barbie doll.

The high-water mark for high-end dolls was reached in 1995 when Mattel introduced the Pink Splendor, a gorgeous doll featuring a spectacular Swarovski crystal-encrusted gown. As equally impressive was its price tag: $900.

The Bob Mackie Era, 1990 – present

*K*NOWN PRIMARILY AS THE MAN WHO DRESSES CHER and other celebrities in vibrant, elaborate and daring fashions, Bob Mackie has excelled for two decades dressing his favorite petite model—Barbie doll—in dream designs. These glitzy dolls, which have always entranced the secondary market, literally drip with sequins, beads and rhinestones.

There's little dispute that the Mackie dolls epitomize glamour, transporting collectors to a fashion world they may never personally inhabit. Even the packaging continues the flavor of the dolls.

Detail is impeccable—nothing less than collectors would expect. Queen of Hearts sports a realistic beauty mark and striking lavender eyes; Starlight Splendor wears peacock-inspired eye shadow; Neptune Fantasy literally swims in flowing sea-colored velvet.

Mackie's Fantasy Goddess series depicted the allure and diversity of ethnic dress from Asia, Africa and other continents. Mackie has also created one-of-a-kind dolls for Mattel's annual Dream Halloween auction.

There is a reason Bob Mackie is called the "Sultan of Sequins." Fitted in a daring gown of 5,000 hand-sewn golden sequins accented with a white feather boa, Bob Mackie's 1990 Limited Edition Gold Barbie doll is a vision of fantasy couture. Her platinum blond hair is pulled up, and accented by a golden headpiece. Golden earrings and bracelets accent this incredible ensemble. The doll retailed for $150.

Released in 1992, Bob Mackie's Empress Bride Barbie doll is considered by many to be the ultimate bride doll in the Barbie Collectibles line. She wears an ivory brocade gown with golden embroidery in a fleur-de-lis design, an expansive layered, pleated tulle skirt, tiara crown with marquis-cut rhinestone and veil, and beaded choker.

Starlight Splendor, Bob Mackie's 1991 Barbie doll exclusive, was a stunning and exotic creation featuring the first African-American Barbie doll in the series. Barbie was spectacular in a fitted black and silvery gown with more than 5,000 hand-sewn sequins and beads, matching silvery headdress and feather train.

A vision of oceanic splendor, Bob Mackie's Neptune Fantasy made a splash in 1992 wearing a blue and green sequined and velvet gown. Her platinum blond hair has a turquoise streak in it, and is tied on top of her head, accented with a turquoise sequined headpiece. This is the first doll in the Mackie collection to feature closed-mouth sculpting.

It is no mystery why Bob Mackie's Masquerade Ball Barbie was a hit in 1993. Wearing a multi-colored harlequin gown of vivid glass bugle beads sewn in diamond patterns, and accented with a velvety black overskirt, Barbie doll was the queen of the ball. Her braided titian hair is topped by an elaborate black hat with feathers.

Bob Mackie's 1994 Queen of Hearts Barbie doll wears a luscious red ensemble featuring a gorgeous sequined gown, heart-embroidered cape, and fanciful headdress, all offset by her stunning features and dark upswept hair.

Moon Goddess Barbie doll wears a shimmering midnight blue sheath covered with sequins in this Bob Mackie offering from 1996. A fanciful "moonbeam" drapes over her shoulder and falls into an elegant floor length cape, accented with stars. Her hair is swept up beneath a deep blue hat and dangling crescent earrings complete the fantasy.

A dazzling offering, Bob Mackie's 1995 Goddess of Sun Barbie doll features a gown encrusted with more than 11,000 sequins and beads. The sparkling ensemble includes a luminous collar and rays of the sun seemingly shoot from her shoulders. Barbie doll's unique, yellow gold hair shines like golden flax above a majestic headpiece accented with rhinestones. Earrings shaped like miniature suns brighten her mysterious smile.

In celebration of Barbie doll's 40th anniversary in 1999, designer Bob Mackie created Le Papillon Barbie — his fantasy image of the shimmering wonder of a butterfly. The doll is draped in a dramatic, full-length, strapless, fitted gown of velvety black with circular train and black stockings. Her slim silhouette is adorned with pink and silvery embroidery, and two shimmering rose-colored rhinestones. Large black butterfly wings with silvery and rose-tinted embroidery, speckled with matching rhinestones coordinate with her dress. An impressive headpiece befitting the bold beauty of a butterfly showcases her radiant pink hair and lavender eyes.

Madame du Barbie doll, Bob Mackie's 1997 Marie Antoinette lookalike, captures the majesty and opulent elegance of the eighteenth century royal court of France. Her gown is a breathtaking confection of ice blue brocade with bead and jewel-embellished rococo embroidery. The coiffure and headpiece are appropriate for the most elegant of royal occasions.

Fantasy Goddess of the Americas from 2000 by Bob Mackie was part of the International Beauty Collection, celebrating the beauty of women from all around the world. Mackie's extravagant fashion style is on full display. The ensemble features ornate beading, sequins, and embroidery in gold, white and aqua tones. Atop Barbie doll's head is a spectacular eagle-inspired headpiece with geometric angles extending down her back. Embroidered bracelets accented with golden beads shimmer on both wrists. Her jet black hair falls in floor-length black braids, accented with golden cord.

Fantasy Goddess of the Arctic was Bob Mackie's 2001 contribution to the International Beauty Collection. Barbie doll's magnificent ensemble, inspired by the Arctic culture, is sure to warm the coldest winter night. Barbie doll wears a long, dramatic dark blue coat, trimmed in faux fur and lined in brilliant fuchsia. The coat is elaborately embroidered, with strands of silvery beads cascading from the hood. Barbie doll's platinum blond hair is pulled up in an intricate hairstyle and decorated with a beautifully beaded headband. Silvery earrings add the finishing touch to this chilling ensemble.

Bob Mackie revealed Radiant Redhead Barbie in 2002, the premier doll in The Red Carpet Collection. This sensational starlet wears a bold white gown that overlaps at the waist and crosses at the chest to reveal a bare mid-riff. Her ensemble features an ornate design of golden edge embroidery, golden beading, and a golden and apple-green pattern that meanders at the edges. With details like luxurious red hair, an over-sized white faux-fur muff reminiscent of classic Hollywood style, a rhinestone hand ring and strappy platform sandals, this starlet is the talk of Tinseltown. Her red carpet runway was a Dealer Exclusive, not sold with doll.

Released in 2003 as part of The Red Carpet Collection, Bob Mackie's Brunette Brilliance Barbie features Barbie doll in a stunning black velvet gown embroidered in silver with pink, purple, and silver beading. A fuchsia overskirt and stand-up notched collar edged in silver beads and silver and black embroidery complete her magnificent ensemble. Rhinestone earrings accent her short black hair against her ultra pale skin.

BARBIE "WEDDING DAY" SET
(without doll) #972

Magnificent church wedding gown with formal train, fashioned for a fairy princess. Tiny mock pearl tiara holds the tiered bridal veil. White satin gown under billowing layers of flowered nylon tulle. Short white nylon gloves, sentimental blue garter, bridal bouquet and white slippers. The set, $5.00.

#972

Despite never being officially married, no one does weddings better than Barbie doll. Bob Mackie's 2006 Couture Confection Bride Barbie doll wearing a fantasy wedding gown as delicate as spun sugar and pretty as a petit four. Inspired by the sweetest of brides, this doll epitomizes Mackie's signature wit, drop-dead style, and over-the-top glamour. The perfect complement for this luscious gown: sparkling Swarovski crystal earrings!

Nostalgic Reproductions, 1994-present

OWNING ORIGINAL VINTAGE BARBIE DOLLS is something every collector aspires to, but with rising prices, scarce supply and steady demand, owning a Barbie doll rarity isn't always realistic.

What, then, could Mattel do to quench collectors' demand for the look and quality of the past?

Beginning in 1994, Mattel issued its first reproduction of a vintage doll as part of its Nostalgic Series collection. Honoring the 35th anniversary of Barbie doll, this was a reproduction of the 1959 #1 Ponytail. While not an exact replica (body markings are different and the packaging is clearly marked as a reproduction), the doll was just close enough to satisfy collectors who cherished the look of the Ponytails (but not their price tag).

Later reproductions featured vintage dolls in popular retro fashions like Silken Flame, Solo in the Spotlight, Busy Gal and Enchanted Evening. In later years, the line was dubbed the Collector's Request Collection, culling their selections from—who better?—avid collectors. Perennial favorites Malibu Barbie and Color Magic Barbie are among the dolls to have been reproduced, much to collectors' delights.

Fashion Luncheon

$\mathcal{B}$EHOLD A VISION IN PINK! This 1997 limited edition Fashion Luncheon reproduction is the only vinyl reproduction of Barbie doll in the popular 1966-67 vintage fashion outfit. From her smart pink ensemble, complete with dress and matching jacket, to her subtle accessories—pink hat, long white tricot gloves and pale pink heels, Barbie doll looks her elegant best.

Evening Splendour

$\mathcal{T}$HIS 2005 REPRODUCTION of Evening Splendour came wearing her matching gold lame coat and sheath dress, and included her short white gloves, turquoise cordoroy bag and hankie, hat with pearl trim and brown open toe heels.

Suburban Shopper

TAKE A SHOPPING TRIP down memory lane with this nostalgic reproduction of the 1959 fashion favorite, Suburban Shopper. Out and about in a wonderful 1950s blue and white striped sun dress, this Barbie doll is the epitome of style from the period. Her fun, straw-like cartwheel hat and handbag with summery "fruits" recall a simpler, sweeter day. A golden chain necklace with a faux-pearl pendant gives the Limited Edition doll a final charming touch.

Picnic Set Barbie

*R*ELEASED IN 2006, PICNIC SET BARBIE doll wears a vintage reproduction of an ensemble originally introduced in 1959. Red and white check shirt, clam-diggers, and straw hat comprise the perfect outfit for a day off, fishing and picnicking. Wedgie sandals, a woven picnic basket, and fishing pole complete this wonderfully nostalgic Barbie doll.

A Color Magic Barbie reproduction comes in the same beautiful diamond print swimsuit as the 1966 original. The yellow and green in the suit changed to red and burgundy as did Barbie doll's matching headband. She also wore turquoise open-toe heels and a turquoise clip in her hair. Other accessories included a card of pink, green, and two blue grosgrain ribbons and yellow, green, pink clips, blue tulle styling net, Color Magic Changer A and B, sponge applicator with pink handle, and instruction booklet.

Released in 1995, this reproduction of the 1965 classic Poodle Parade fashion outfit is part of the popular Collectors' Request Collection. Barbie doll wears a fitted olive jumper, a line pink dickey with turtleneck, a green and white checkerboard print knit coat with pink knit edging and pink cotton lining. Barbie doll also came with an olive green tote bag, a metal trophy and a Poodle Parade First Prize certificate.

Billions of Dreams, 1997

*J*UST HOW MANY DREAMS has the Barbie doll inspired? Why, billions, of course! This striking limited-edition doll, with upswept hair, Swarovski crystal earrings and icy blue dress, was created to commemorate just that concept. The doll was a glimmering tribute to everything Mattel had hoped for with Barbie doll—that the dreams of billions of girls would be personified through their creation. This stunning doll features a beautiful gown in icy blue satin and sparkling with "jewels." Under her full skirt and train is a full petticoat of palest pink tulle. Her accessories include satin panties, satin shawl, quilted purse, blue spike heels and crystal drop earrings. Her platinum blond hair is upswept in a glamorous hair style accented with light bangs.

Pink Splendor, 1997

THIS LIMIT-EDITION GODDESS—only 10,000 dolls were produced worldwide—wore an exquisite pale pink gown of fine silk satin trimmed in a delicate, glittering lace. The bodice was made of golden lace over pale pink taffeta, accented beautifully with shimmering rhinestones. A wide pink ribbon formed a bow in the back that flowed down into a extravagant train. The back of her gown was adorned with graceful pink roses while crystal jewelry added a regal charm. Her accessories included pink silk panties, iridescent stockings and lovely pink garters. Her dramatic hairstyle added to her grand appearance. With that said, however, the most striking aspect of the doll was her price tag: $900.

Harley-Davidson Line, 1996-present

TAKE ONE LONGTIME MOTORCYCLE SUCCESS STORY. Add the beauty of Barbie dolls. Toss in a sassy dose of leather and denim . . . and hit the open road! The perfect marriage of the two revered brand names was destined to be a hit.

No longer were motorcycles just for "bikers." This series illustrates the mainstream acceptance of Harley-Davidson. Popularized by Jay Leno and other recognizable celebs, the bikes became touted as American classics, almost as much as mom and apple pie.

It's tough enough to imagine a line of Barbie dolls released in any earlier decade being associated with motorcycles and leather jackets and being Toys R Us exclusives, to boot.

Few licenses have such strong name recognition as Harley-Davidson, and even fewer hold the power to pair up with a powerhouse such as Barbie doll. The marriage, however, spawned seven dolls (five Barbie dolls and two Ken dolls) and a miniature Harley-Davidson Fat Boy motorcycle.

The Phantom of the Opera Gift Set was an FAO Schwarz exclusive in 1998.

The Star Trek Barbie and Ken 30th Anniversary Gift Set, 1996.

Barbie and Ken Gift Sets

GIFT SETS FEATURING BARBIE DOLL AND KEN DOLL have been offered for more than 35 years. The earliest sets, from the mid-1960s, paired the duo as parade leaders (the 1964 On Parade gift set) and bride and groom (Wedding Party also issued in 1964).

It wasn't until the 1990s, however, that gift sets featuring the two were aimed directly at collectors. These sets became increasingly more creative as Barbie and Ken morphed into TV stars (Star Trek, 1996; X-Files, 1998; Morticia and Gomez Addams, 2000), literary lovers (Romeo and Juliet, 1998; Phantom of the Opera, 1998) and mystical, magical pairs (King Arthur and Queen Guinevere, 1999; Merlin and Morgan LeFay, 2000; Sultan and Scheherazade, 2001).

1990s

97

Autumn in Paris Barbie doll was introduced in 1998 as part of the City Seasons Collection.

Unveiled in 1999, Winter in Montreal Barbie doll is outfitted for beauty and warmth in her red A-line swing coat with black fringe shawl collar. A matching slim skirt and black vinyl belt pairs perfectly with leopard print shell and matching print faux fur hand muff.

Series Dolls

*T*HIS WAS TRULY THE DECADE of the collector series–enticing consumers to buy not just one, but all the dolls to complete the series. Attractive packaging added to the dolls' display value. Among the series debuting during this time were the extremely popular Children's Collector Series, an homage to popular children's characters, such as Little Bo Peep, Cinderella, Rapunzel and Sleeping Beauty.

Another series that drew interest—especially because it took buyers on vicarious globetrotting adventures—was the City Seasons series. This series spotlighted not just romantic venues–such as Tokyo and Rome–but the stylish apparel Barbie doll would wear during her seasonal travels.

Visions of strolling down Fifth Avenue come to mind with Winter in New York Barbie doll. Released in 1998, the always fashionable Barbie managed to keep the Manhattan chill at bay.

Spring in Tokyo Barbie
doll was released in 1999
and featured the classic
fashion outfit that has
come to define Barbie.

#1 Lingerie Barbie doll carried a decidedly daring look and ravishingly brash attitude in 2000. Part of the Fashion Model Collection, Barbie doll wore a white satin bra and panty ensemble trimmed with white lace and pale pink bows, white stockings and garters.

CHAPTER 6

Barbie Moves Back to the Future

$\mathcal{T}$HE BEGINNING OF THE NEW MILLENNIUM brought many innovative and exciting developments to Barbie doll's world. Yet the new decade also saw the doll return to her roots as a fashion model with a sophisticated look.

The aptly named Fashion Model Series revealed one of the most impressive and daring Barbie dolls of all time, Lingerie Barbie doll. Even though what Barbie doll was wearing was eye-catching and provocative, what she was made of proved to be revolutionary.

The Fashion Model Series introduced Silkstone, a new material Mattel used offering the weight, look and feel of a porcelain doll.

Of course, Silkstone would not have been so revolutionary if Barbie doll didn't look spectacular, which she did. From scantily clad beauties to Pop Culture superstars, Barbie doll radiated unparalleled beauty at the dawning of a new era.

Barbie no longer was a teenage fashion model, and she didn't wear that wonderfully hip black-and-white striped swimsuit from the 1950s. Yet she was definitely of those times. The more Barbie matured, the more she seemed to remind everyone from where she had come. More than fifty years after Ruth Handler had forever changed the world of play for little girls, Barbie doll continues to evolve and impress, always pushing the boundaries of possibilities.

Fashion Model Series, 2000

*T*HE MILLENNIUM MAY HAVE COME in on little cat feet, but Barbie doll was roaring like a tiger. And it was obvious Mattel had put a lot of time, research and design into its newest model for her walk down the 21st-century catwalk.

The Fashion Model Series, made from the magical Silkstone material, seemed to move Barbie doll forward while giving a nod to her wonderful beginnings. Since 1959, "fashion" has remained Barbie doll's middle name. Retro in flavor (in both look and fashions), these dolls returned—if not literally at least figuratively—to Barbie doll's roots while unveiling her as a supermodel for the millennium. They recall the demeanor, style and eloquence of movie stars like Grace Kelly and Veronica Lake. They had a decidedly daring look, a ravishingly brash attitude and a revolutionary new material. How could they miss?

Two lingerie dolls initially kicked off the line, while later dolls were dressed in nighttime elegance ranging from robes and chemises to stunning evening wear.

An air of magic, mystery and glamour surrounds the typical Hollywood soiree, and who better to capture Tinseltown's glory days than 2007's Movie Mixer Barbie doll? This blond beauty is every bit the sweet, enchanting starlet in a simple, satiny dress of dusty rose. The demure look is accentuated by a matching pink purse, hair ribbon and heels, while faux pearls and white elbow-length gloves add a dazzling dose of drama, giving Movie Mixer Barbie doll unmistakable movie star style.

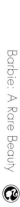

This FAO Schwarz Exclusive Joyeux Barbie doll, released in 2004, wears a dazzling gown perfect for any holiday occasion. A fitted white satin and organza strapless gown is clouded over with a dramatic, detachable overskirt. For added shimmer, silvery sequins and faux pearls adorn this snowy-white showstopper. A rhinestone tiara and drop earrings complete the festive mood. Joyeux Barbie doll was the first-ever Holiday doll created for the Silkstone Collection.

This ultra limited edition Chataine Barbie doll, a 2003 FAO Schwarz Exclusive, is dressed in a creamy cappuccino-colored evening ensemble consisting of a strapless taffeta bustier and mermaid skirt. A taupe organza evening jacket embroidered with golden sequins and lace trim highlights this dazzling mix. A luxurious chocolate brown faux fur stole adds richness. Golden and rhinestone drop earrings play beautifully against her brunette hair styled in an intricate evening chignon. A Blond doll Capucine Barbie doll was also issued this same year, wearing this same ensemble as Chantine.

Barbie Fashion Model Collection celebrated Barbie doll's 45th anniversary in 2004. Barbie doll wears a dramatic black gown, joyously graffiti printed in pink and white. Ken doll joins the fun in a white dinner jacket with classic black tuxedo pants. Included in this Limited Edition gift set is a signed sketch of this BFMC 45th Anniversary Barbie doll. Three versions of Barbie were available for a very lucky Ken doll.

Released in 2005, Trace of Lace Barbie doll is completely elegant in a dress of black lace and chiffon, featuring a skirt with tiers of feminine ruffles. Jet-black beads add delicate embellishment, while satin ribbon accents the bodice and waist. A golden and rhinestone brooch and golden, rhinestone and faux pearl bracelet lend an air of opulence. Sheer black hose, black satin clutch purse, and black heels are the elegant final touches. The Platinum Label version (in box) of the Gold Label brunette edition of A Trace of Lace Barbie

Fresh as the English countryside, Lady of the Manor Barbie doll wears a lovely strapless white gown embellished with extravagant floral embroidery work, faux pearls, and Swarovski crystals. Elegant white opera length gloves and a sheer stole lend an air of dramatic style. A golden brooch, worn at the waist, and stud earrings are the final wonderful accessories. Designer Robert Best beautifully captures the posh life in this 2006 release.

Every spring should produce such a beautiful flower as Violette Barbie doll. This 2006 dealer exclusive, limited to 999 dolls produced worldwide, joins the Barbie Fashion Model Collection dressed for a stylish ball. She wears a gown made of printed silk organza over a satin under dress and tulle petticoat with lilac taffeta trim. It's a springtime vision of the ultimate romantic, retro ball gown and finished with violets in her hair.

2000s

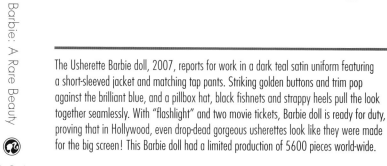

Released in 2007, Hollywood Hostess Barbie doll is the epitome of effortless chic. Dressed in a palette of soothing, simple hues, this doll raises the bar for California-casual style. A tangerine chiffon sash, tied beautifully at the waist, balances the lacy white top and pants, while aqua jewelry brings the glam factor up a notch. The doll's side-swept red curls add another lovely splash of color to this stunning look. Additional accessories include a tangerine jumpsuit with white belt, a white lace skirt and a silvery "tea set" complete with spoons, cups and saucers for four, plus a sugar bowl, creamer and tea pot.

Barbie
Fashion Model
COLLECTION

all my Best
Robert Best
6·30·07

The Usherette
Genuine Silkstone™ Body

BARBIE B COLLECTOR

The Usherette Barbie doll, 2007, reports for work in a dark teal satin uniform featuring a short-sleeved jacket and matching tap pants. Striking golden buttons and trim pop against the brilliant blue, and a pillbox hat, black fishnets and strappy heels pull the look together seamlessly. With "flashlight" and two movie tickets, Barbie doll is ready for duty, proving that in Hollywood, even drop-dead gorgeous usherettes look like they were made for the big screen! This Barbie doll had a limited production of 5600 pieces world-wide.

𝒜LL THE CRITICS AGREE: the newest star of the silver screen is a show-stopper in every sense! And she knows exactly how to make a grand entrance in a retro-glam ensemble of bold animal prints and shots of brilliant red. In true movie star style, Red Hot Reviews Barbie doll (2007) is stunning in a gorgeous belted dress, dramatic cape, and flawlessly matching handbag. Red-hot heels kick it up a notch, and oversized sunglasses are the final must-have in this unforgettably immaculate, devastatingly glamorous look. Not to be outdone, Barbie doll is resplendent in her Dusk to Dawn outfit from 2001.

Barbie Loves Pop Culture

*I*F ONE NOTABLE SHIFT TOOK PLACE at the turn of the last century, it was a boom in the number of pop culture properties the Barbie doll world embraced. There was hardly an entertainment property Barbie didn't touch, and Mattel even named a series Barbie Loves Pop Culture.

The dolls made the most of licensing ties—teaming with comic book properties, popular films and television shows. Often, Barbie, and sometimes Ken, was morphing into her favorite characters. It wasn't a new concept entirely. In the 1990s, Barbie and Ken gift sets and the Harley-Davidson line used the concept as well. But never was pop culture more prevalent as in the doll's most recent decade.

Among the dolls that had collectors buzzing were comic properties including Batgirl, Black Canary, Super Girl and Wonder Woman.

Pictured is Jeannie, from *I Dream of Jeannie*, as Barbie doll. She is part of the Barbie Loves Pop Culture line from 2001.

Elle Woods is back for another fun romp in *Legally Blond 2: Red, White and Blond.* And donning her own set of sassy sandals, Barbie doll makes the ultimate tribute to this icon of feminine style as Barbie as Elle Woods. Dressed in Elle's trademark pink suit complete with a special matching ensemble for her beloved dog, this doll captures all the signature details that made Elle's look so popular in the original blockbuster hit, Legally Blond. Barbie is accessorized with tiny pearl earrings and a matching double strand pearl necklace that are reminiscent of the Mikimoto necklace and earrings seen in the film. This doll, issued in 2003 was part of Barbie Loves Pop Culture.

Holy Hot Stuff, Batman, Barbie doll sure makes a beautiful Batgirl. Released in 2008, Batgirl Barbie doll would drive even Ken doll batty enough to commit a crime just so he could be lucky enough to be captured by her.

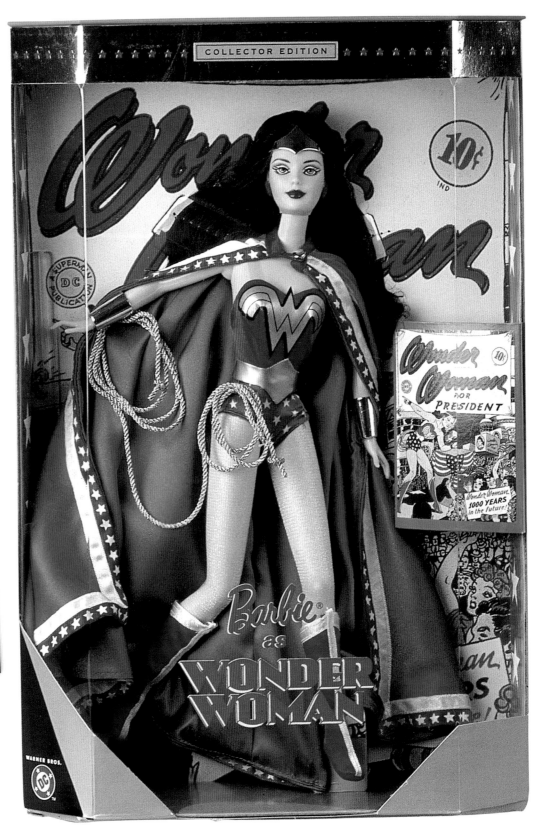

After being a hero to little girls for four decades, Barbie doll finally became a super-hero in 2000. Dressed in an authentic reproduction of a Wonder Woman costume inspired by the popular comic book hero, Barbie doll made it a crime not to look fabulous.

Designers' World

FOR DECADES, BARBIE'S WORLD had been inhabited by designers who worked with real models—but they were all to willing to transform their elegant designs to Barbie doll size. But after the turn of the century, it seems just about every designer was clamoring to have their work modeled by America's original fashion model.

Dressing Barbie doll in the 21st century were notable designers including Cynthia Rowley, Badgely Mischka, Monique Lhuillier, Reem Acra Lilly Pulitzer, Judith Leiber, Anna Sui, Kate Spade, Zac Posen, Paul Frank and others.

Cynthia Rowley was only 7 when she designed her first dress and a senior in art school when she sold her first collection of 8 pieces. The award-winning designer's line includes heels, menswear, jeans, accessories, as well as a signature fragrance. Released in 2005, the Cynthia Rowley Barbie doll is fun, flirty and incredibly feminine and was designed by Katina Jimenez, who also worked on Kate Spade and Giorgio Armani.

Released in 2004, the Kate Spade Barbie doll is dressed in an outfit that reflects the designer's personal style. The doll wears a floral print coat with three-quarter length sleeves, belted at the waist. Beneath the coat is an ivory knit sweater and green shantung cigarette pants. A faux wicker handbag with golden detail is reminiscent of Kate's handbag designs, specifically the "Venice Basket." Barbie doll also carries a "canvas" tote trimmed with faux green leather. The dog perched at the edge of the bag is modeled after Kate's own dog. Barbie doll has many striking accessories including a beaded necklace and earring set with faux turquoise accents and oversized sunglasses.

Released in 2005, Carolina Herrera Bride Barbie doll wears an elegant gown, perfect for the most romantic wedding. Part of the Designer Brides Collection, this stunning Barbie doll wears a beautiful, beaded gown featuring ecru corded lace. The bodice is crisscrossed with satin-edged organza ribbon. The veil of off-white tulle is edged with lace and embellished with faux pearls. Pretty blue ribbons decorate the shoes. A white rose bouquet and earrings complete this bridal beauty.

#0947

BRIDE'S DREAM

Traditional white satin wedding gown with nylon chiffon overskirt and ruffles down the front panel from the waist. Tiny mock pearl tiara holds tulle bridal veil. Long white gloves, single strand pearl necklace, sentimental blue garter, bridal bouquet and white slippers. (without doll) $3.50

Released in 2005, this Platinum Edition Judith Leiber Barbie doll takes to the red carpet. A timeless classic that's always in fashion, the name Judith Leiber inspires a dazzling doll perfect for the spotlight or candlelight. The stunning ensemble includes a strapless cocktail dress of taupe lace with a scalloped hem. Her full skirt and fitted corset are accented with tiny golden sequins.

Say adios to the ordinary! Introduced in 2006, Dahlia was a Platinum Dealer Exclusive limited to 999 total pieces produced. Influenced by the exotic romanticism of Spain, Dahlia Barbie doll wears a lovely strapless gown of white on black lace. Designed by Robert Best, this red-headed beauty shines in satiny white opera gloves, silvery earrings and a brooch embellished with Swarovski crystals. Olé!

Awards night is here, and there's a red-headed stunner making waves on the red carpet and beyond. Another gorgeous creation from designer Robert Best, 2007's The Siren Barbie doll is every bit the enchantress, heating up the silver screen with cascading red curls and a hypnotic gaze. In a strapless black mermaid gown that recalls the glamour of old Hollywood, our sizzling starlet is the picture of perfection and mystique.

Barbie doll as
fashion designer
in the lovely
Busy Gal outfit
released in 1960.

CHAPTER 7

Occupation Sensation
Barbie's World of Careers

*W*HAT'S A GIRL TO DO? Just about anything she wants. In fact, "be anything" became a marketing slogan for Barbie doll. Since Barbie could be anything, little girls could vicariously do so as well. Barbie illustrated just what was possible. After all, she has tried more than 80 careers through the years.

Naturally, Barbie doll's early work life matched the career trajectories of the times. At first billed as a "teen-age fashion model," she soon found herself working as a nurse, student teacher, ballerina or fashion model—most were traditional female roles of their day. The fact is, Mattel was deeply in tune with the spirit of the times whenever they created a new identity or opportunity for the Barbie doll.

In many ways, however, Barbie doll was ahead of her time. She was a college graduate in 1963; a business executive in 1986; a "Summit Diplomat" and airline pilot in 1990; and a presidential candidate in 1992. Consider that she was an astronaut in 1965, nearly 20 years before Sally Ride became America's first woman in space aboard the Space Shuttle Challenger in 1983.

Barbie doll has had her share of great jobs throughout the years. She's become a superhero (Wonder Woman), NASCAR driver, rock star, paleontologist and concert pianist, just to name a few.

Stylish & Professional

*B*ARBIE THE "TEENAGE FASHION MODEL" became Barbie the "Fashion Designer" in this stunning Busy Gal (#981) ensemble from 1960. Showcased by #6 Redhead Ponytail Barbie doll, this wonderful outfit was stylish and professional. Barbie doll had a touch of fashion and intelligence in black-rimmed glasses and a red linen suit. Her sheath skirt was topped by a short-sleeved jacket with red and white striped facing that matched her halter body blouse. Contrast was found in the accessories: blue straw open crown hat with stripe lining matching her body blouse, matching blue straw belt lined in red. Navy open-toe heels finished her "dressed for success" look. The entire outfit, including two black-and-white illustrations found in her portfolio, continued to advance the "woman-as-career-professional" theme of the doll.

Fashion Editor Barbie doll, 2001, from the Fashion Model Collection.

Politically Correct

$\mathcal{H}$OW DO YOU MAKE A POLITICAL STATEMENT while remaining nonpartisan? In an election year, you introduce your own candidate—and who has more name recognition than the Barbie doll? Barbie doll's initial run for the White House came during the heated race between George Bush, Bill Clinton and Ross Perot. Barbie as President, a Toys R Us exclusive for 1992, may not have had a platform, but she did have moxie. She was so confident of her chances of winning that she wore a star-spangled red, white and blue gown for the inaugural ball. This doll was a positive sign of the times, allowing Mattel to bridge the complicated and controversial world of politics with a candidate everyone could stand behind.

School Days

SKIPPER AND A VERY RARE Brownette Bubblecut Barbie doll are ready for the first day of school in their coordinating School Girl/Student Teacher outfits. Barbie doll looked forward to her student teaching venture in the 6th grade geography class in her 1965 Student Teacher (#1622) outfit. Her outfit featured a red knit bodice with white tuck front inset with collar and two red shank buttons. The skirt was red and white hounds-tooth accented by a slim red shiny plastic belt at the dropped waistline. Red high heel closed-toe heels and black-framed glasses completed her glamorous scholastic look. Her schoolroom accessories included a plastic blue and black plastic globe, a black pointer with silver tip and a blue geography book. Skipper's School Girl (#1921) outfit featured a pleated skirt of the same hounds-tooth fabric. A white sleeveless blouse with collar has red stitching and two shank buttons detailing the front. The red cardigan jacket featured a crest on the hip pocket. Her scholastic accessories included Brown Eyeglasses, a red wax apple with red and green painted accents and a short, black shiny plastic book-strap that held three books and a red and a brown wooden pencil.

Come Fly with Me

ʙUBBLECUT BARBIE DOLL'S FUTURE appears sky high wearing this American Airlines Stewardess (#984) outfit from 1961. A smart authentic fitted suit in navy blue features a trim jacket with silver metal wings and four button closure. The sheath skirt topped a sheer white nylon body blouse with collar and three-button front. Barbie doll doll's matching hat features the American Airlines insignia in silver metal. Her zippered navy flight bag features "American Airlines" and the insignia in white. Finishing touches include a black plastic shoulder bag and matching black open-toe heels.

AMERICAN AIRLINES

Clinically Approved

$\mathcal{H}$EALTH CARE CAN PROVIDE a wonderfully rewarding career, as Barbie doll and friends demonstrated in the early 1960s. Here, Dr. Ken, looking as if he stepped out of a scene from television's *Dr. Kildare,* is joined by Midge (left) wearing a Japanese exclusive Candy Striper Volunteer outfit and Registered Nurse Barbie doll. Barbie doll even came with a diploma that declared her as a Nursing School graduate.

Released in 2006, The Nurse Barbie doll, designed by Robert Best, celebrated the working woman. The uniform included a crisp white, belted dress, matching cap, and blue cape. White mary janes complete the ensemble. The AA version was a Barbie Fan Club Exclusive doll limited to 999 pieces world-wide.

Career Chic

$\mathcal{T}$HE BARBIE FASHION MODEL Collection made even the most modest of careers stylish. Part of the Gold Label Collection, these Silkstone lovelies are not only stunning but in short supply, with limited production runs. Here, Barbie doll appears (from left with production numbers) in a 2006 Canadian exclusive as a French Maid (5,200); in a 2008 exclusive to Singapore as a Teacher (5,300); in a 2006 U.S. exclusive as a Waitress (13,400); in a 2006 Japanese exclusive as a Stewardess (3,900); and in a Canadian exclusive as a Secretary (8,100).

Barbie doll was practically born to wear
pink. And wearing 1960's Enchanted
Evening (#983) she looked unforgettable
in this famous pale pink satin gown.

CHAPTER 8

Fashion Forward
Style Through the Decades

*E*VEN THOUGH THE FIRST BARBIE DOLL was introduced to buyers in a now-famous black-and-white swimsuit, it was obvious from that moment that Barbie was destined to become a fashion plate. Although her swimwear was utilitarian and far from trendy, she would soon model outfits that embodied elegance, glamour, professionalism and an adventurous spirit.

Most early Barbie dolls donned the zebra-stripe swimsuit and were packaged in regular-issue boxes. Some of these dolls, however, were found in "pink silhouette" boxes (a pale pink box with silhouetted figures of the dolls on the front). Early Ponytail dolls were dressed in outfits and placed in these boxes for store display only and were never intended to be sold. These special dolls were used to highlight the new Barbie doll dressed in her fashion. Some of Barbie doll's most stylish (and now most cherished) outfits were modeled in these boxes.

Barbie doll's fashion catalog is epic and well-rounded. Such early classic outfits like Gay Parisienne, Roman Holiday and Easter Parade came to define Barbie doll's fashion beginnings. Throughout the decades, Barbie doll's fashions have echoed the trends in society—from the buttoned up and fancy fare of the 1960s to the mod-era designs of the 1970s, the frilly 1980s, the designer 1990s and the daring and edgier looks of the 21st century Fashion Model series.

*T*HE POUFY BUBBLE DRESS of Gay Pariesienne (#964) from 1959 is a classic of Barbie doll fashion. Worn by #2 Blond Ponytail Barbie doll, the outfit depicts the high style of the times. The dress was fashioned in deep blue pin-dot rayon taffeta with accent bows edged in white. These bows adorned the hem in front and the top of the zipper closing in the back. Many accessories included a glamorous veiled headband hat in matching blue tulle. A fluffy "Barbie" labeled faux fur stole with white satin lining, long white tricot gloves, and blue open-toe heels added more excitement to the evening look. No outfit was complete without jewelry and in this case, a graduated strand of faux pearls and matching earrings served the purpose. A small gold velvet clutch with gold bead closure, lined in white satin completed the ensemble.

*W*EARING ONE OF THE MOST coveted vintage outfits, #3 Brunette Ponytail Barbie doll is resplendent in Easter Parade (#971) from 1959. The apple print, polished cotton sheath dress (identical to the Apple Print Sheath Set #917, genuine Easter Parade Sheath does not have a Barbie clothing label) combined with a smart black faille unlined spring coat. The back gathered into the yoke and the big patch pockets had self-bow accents. Barbie doll's headband hat was a simple bow fashioned from silk organza. Other accessories included a black patent clutch bag, graduated pearl necklace, matching earrings, short white tricot gloves and black open-toe heels.

THE FANCY OF MANY a southern gentleman, a lovely #1 Blond Ponytail Barbie doll wears the 1959-released Plantation Belle (#966). Her waltz-length party dress in pink sheer dot fabric with lace and soutache braid between tiers and around the neck topped a white nylon petticoat with tulle ruffles and single ribbon accent. A large hat with straw crown, woven brim and flower bud accents kept the southern sun out of Barbie doll's eyes. A matching straw purse with sequin and bead accents, graduated pink pearls, matching bracelet and pink pearl earrings, short white tricot gloves, and pale pink open-toe heels completed the outfit.

Fashion-Forward

131

$\mathcal{F}$OUND ONLY IN THE 1959 CATALOG, the classic clean lines of Roman Holiday (#968) make this Barbie doll fashion a timeless favorite. Modeled on #3 Blond Ponytail Barbie doll, the red straw cord half-hat with cord bow in back was easily lost and can be difficult for collectors to find. But without doubt, the rarest accessory included was the tiny brass compact that was no more than 3/8 of an inch in diameter with pink puff tucked inside of compact. Other accessories included a "pearl" on chain necklace, white short tricot gloves, and black open-toe heels. Roman Holiday also came with a white plastic purse with gold bead closure, black-rimmed glasses in a white and clear plastic case, pink plastic comb and hankie.

$\mathcal{B}$ARBIE DOLL INVENTOR RUTH HANDLER BELIEVED in working outside the home and 1959's Commuter Set (#916)—worn here by #4 Brunette Ponytail Barbie doll—reflected that forward-thinking attitude. The collarless navy cardigan in the style of Chanel topped a matching sheath skirt with side zipper and shank button closure. Two blouses for versatility were included with the outfit. For a day at the office, a casual nylon blue and white mini-check body blouse with collar and single button; for an elegant dinner suit look, Barbie doll chose her white satin sleeveless body blouse. A three-flower silk hat was available in red or a bright rose. The opening cardboard hatbox came in red with black cord handle. The Barbie signature was followed by a ™ in earliest sets and by an ® in later ones.

ANOTHER CLASSIC RELEASED IN 1959/1960, Apple Print Sheath (#917) was one of the more figure-flattering outfits of the vintage era. Modeled here by #6 Blond Ponytail Barbie doll, the dress was made of polished cotton and was black with a colorful apple print in red, blue, and green. It also came with rolled collar and back zipper. Simple black open-toe heels completed the look. This same dress was also used in Easter Parade. Dresses found with the "Barbie" clothing label are considered Apple Print Sheath while dresses without the inside label belong to Easter Parade.

Hallmark Keepsake Ornament, Barbie: Solo in the Spotlight, 2nd edition (1995)

Barbie® TEEN AGE FASHION MODEL

#882 "SOLO IN THE SPOTLIGHT"
DRESSED DISPLAY DOLL
(COSTUME ONLY: #982)
© 1958 BY MATTEL, INC.

MATTEL INTERNATIONAL

$\mathcal{F}$RIDAY NIGHT FUN WITH FRIENDS and Ken was an important part of Barbie doll's world in 1960, making the fashion outfit Friday Night Date (#979) an indispensable part of the Barbie doll wardrobe. Here, two Bublecut Barbie dolls model U.S. (left) and Japanese versions of the outfit. Both versions combine the look of a puffed-sleeve blouse with a jumper featuring a full swing skirt. While the jumper and heels differ, both versions feature the same black plastic tray and two drink glasses with painted orange contents. The two tiny solid plastic straws were lost easily and make for great collector finds.

Hallmark Keepsake
Ornament, Barbie:
Enchanted Evening,
3rd edition (1996)

*B*ARBIE DOLL IS SOPHISTICATED and charming in 1960's
Enchanted Evening (#983). The bodice had a fold-over hem at
the top. The skirt was slim with a long, draping train at her left
side. At the waist there was a fabric rose or three sequins with
three beads accent. A white rabbit fur stole with pink satin
lining warmed Barbie doll's shoulders. Accessories included
long white tricot gloves, three row pearl choker with two pearl
drops at closure, matching earrings with pearl drops, and
clear open-toe heels with gold glitter at the toe and heel.

*L*IFE IS A HIGHWAY and this Redhead Bubblecut Barbie dolls proves that the adventure can be chic. Barbie doll hit the open road in 1961's aptly titled Open Road (#985) outfit. Her smart traveling fashion featured slim slacks in a red/black/gray stripe with back zipper. A beige wool short-sleeved shell sweater with back closure topped the pants, along with a matching khaki car coat with functioning toggles lined in a striped fabric. Barbie doll's straw hat attached to a red chiffon scarf that tied under her chin. (The hatband was of the matching red chiffon.) She added a pair of red rimmed/blue lens sunglasses and cork wedgies with red "patent" uppers and of course her very own Road Map.

$\mathcal{T}$URNING HEADS WAS EASY for this Blond Bubblecut Barbie doll in 1962's Red Flare (#939), a rich red velvet tent coat. The sleeves puff and push up to a three-quarter length over long white tricot gloves. The coat was lined in rich white satin, as was the matching clutch bag. A red velvet pillbox hat and red open-toe heels completed the look. Opening the coat revealed her Silken Flame (#977) outfit, consisting of a white satin skirt and a red velvet fitted bodice.

*T*ICKETS TO THE LATEST Broadway play require just the right outfit. Thankfully this #5 Blond Ponytail Barbie doll has just the thing: 1963's Theatre Date (#959), an elegant emerald green evening suit. Smart and spectacular, the sheath skirt featured a peplum and was topped off by a matching wide-collared bolero and pillbox hat with bow accent. A white satin sleeveless blouse added a contrasting touch. Emerald green open-toe heels finished the look.

Japanese Pink Silhouette Dressed Box, New Midge

*H*ERE IS AN ITEM RARELY seen as this particular doll is so incredibly rare to find especially in larger version pink store display boxes. Japanese Midge has a unique gentle expression with her sultry side glance brown eyes and small pink lips and no freckles. She has brown molded hair with a blue band and her trademark brunette wig is lovely. Midge comes dressed in a beautiful "Sophisticated Lady" ensemble including long white gloves, clear glittered crown, pink pearl earrings and pink open-toe heels. She comes in her special extra large Pink Silhouette Box. This doll sold for $3,190 in a Doll Attic auction.

EW OF BARBIE DOLL'S OUTFITS featured the detail and workmanship of 1963's Sophisticated Lady (#993). Modeled by #5 Ponytail Barbie doll with factory up-do, the ensemble featured a wide velvet coat fully lined in pink with stand-up collar. The substantial skirt on the silk dress had silver tone filigree lace trim, as did the bodice. The accessories included a strand of pink pearls, long white tricot gloves, pink open-toe heels, and a tiara.

$\mathcal{R}$ESERVATIONS HAVE BEEN MADE for a fabulous evening for Bubblecut Barbie doll in 1963's Dinner at Eight (#946). Her silk hostess pajama ensemble was topped by a gold sparkled burnt orange hostess coat with sweeping skirt. Cute pale tan cork wedgies with metallic gold uppers completed the sophisticated look.

A 1964 RELEASE, KNITTING PRETTY (#957) came in three variations; the soft pink variation is the hardest of the three sets for collectors to find. The outfit featured matching wool cardigan and shell sweaters. A flannel skirt and open-toe heels completed the look. Her knitting accessories included a red cover "How To Knit" book by Barbie, wooden bowl with glued-in yarn in pink, yellow, and green, needles and a pair of functional scissors.

Aɴʏ SOCIAL GATHERING was made spectacular in 1965's Holiday Dance (#1639). American Girl Barbie doll is resplendent in this gold and white striped lamé fabric gown. A gold and white striped lamé fabric formed this beautiful ball gown. The skirt was full and the bodice featured gold braid straps. The bright orange chiffon sash had a hook and thread closing and two rows of gold beads at the closure. Long white tricot gloves, white closed-toe heels and a gold clutch completed the ensemble.

A RARE EUROPEAN PINK version of 1965's glamorous Midnight Blue (#1617) is a sensational look for American Girl Barbie doll. The gown features a lamé strapless bodice that shimmered into the extra full skirt. The cape was generous in fabric that gathered into a white satin-lined fake white fur collar. The fabric in the cape was midnight pink satin with a full satin lining. Long white tricot gloves, graduated pearl necklace, silver clutch bag, and open-toe heels completed the sophisticated ensemble. Midnight Pink has never been shown in any fashion booklets, hence the name and stock number has never been discovered. This fashion originally was sold on a doll in plastic wrapping, at a very low price and is extrememly rare to acquire. Also produced for the Japanese market was Midnight Red which came in Red Satin. Midnight Pink was originally sold without accessories.

Wedding Belles

Although BARBIE DOLL AND KEN DOLL were never officially married, it didn't stop little girls from dressing their favorite dolls in beautiful bridal outfits. Here, a Ponytail Barbie doll wears a 1963 Bride's Dream (#947); an American Girl wears 1966's Here Comes the Bride (#1665); a Bubblecut Barbie doll wears the 1959 classic from Wedding Day set (#972); and Skipper wears a 1966 Junior Bride's Maid outfit (#1934). Ken doll wears a 1961 Tuxedo (#787).

$\mathcal{I}$N 1965'S GOLD 'N GLAMOUR (#1647), American Girl Barbie doll wears a fabulous golden tweed jacket with cape sleeves and four decorative buttons, a matching golden tweed skirt with a striking aqua blue chiffon top, and numerous fun accessories. A matching scarf and hat with rich brown fur trim complemented, long brown tricot gloves unique to this outfit. A foil dimpled purse, graduated pearl necklace and closed-toe heels complete her ensemble.

LIMITED EDITION

Barbie®
*Fashion
Model*

COLLECTION

Sandi,

All my Best

Robert Best

10 · 11 · 02

Lingerie

Genuine Silkstone™ Body

*F*ASHION TOOK A PROVOCATIVE TURN with Lingerie Barbie doll in 2002, who was part of the Barbie Fashion Model Collection. Lingerie Barbie #5 was the first African-American Silkstone doll. Her enchanting ensemble features a delicate black merry widow bustier with pink bow accent. Her matching robe offers alluring cover. Golden hoop earrings and high heels complete this simple but elegant ensemble.

Is it hot in here or is it just Barbie? Difficult to say with 2003's Lingerie Barbie #6, who turns up the heat in a short pearl-grey satin slip trimmed in black lace. Her thigh-high stockings add a touch of excitement while a simple black ribbon bow in Barbie doll's long, straight red hair finishes the look.

Barbie and Midge became best friends in 1963. Here Barbie and Midge both adorn Japanese issued fashions.

CHAPTER 9

We Are Family
Barbie's Circle of Friends

WHILE BARBIE INVENTOR RUTH HANDLER admitted to being somewhat of a loner growing up, that didn't mean Barbie doll was going to be as well. Far from it. Everyone needs a few good friends—even America's favorite doll. Best friends enhance our world and allow us to "just be." Barbie doll's friends did just that.

Two years after Barbie doll was introduced, boyfriend Ken appeared. The freshly-scrubbed Ken doll—adding a much needed Y chromosome to the Barbie doll world—was a dapper escort.

Once Barbie had a boyfriend, she needed a best friend to talk about him with, not to mention someone to share clothes and adventures. Enter Midge in 1963. In 1964 Midge got her own boyfriend, Allan, who just happened to be best friends with Ken. It is, after all, a small world.

Barbie doll's little sister Skipper hit the scene in 1964. Because she was three inches shorter than Barbie doll, Skipper had her own clothing line, with many pieces coordinated with her big sister's. In short order, Skipper acquired two friends, Skooter and Ricky. Tutti and Todd, Barbie doll's "tiny sister and brother," were produced in 1966.

The biggest thing to hit the family, however, was cousin Francie, who in 1966 ushered in the "Mod" fashion scene to Barbie's world. Less shapely than her cousin, Francie was the perfect size to wear all the mod fashions then in vogue. Over time many more celebrities, friends and family would follow, all making the World of Barbie that much more interesting.

WHEN LOVE
COMES TO TOWN
Ken, 1961

Black Barbie and Ken Case.

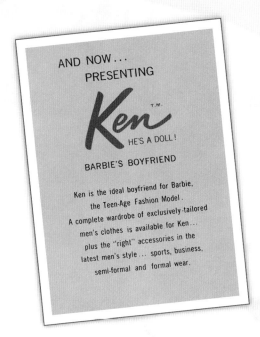

A SINGLE GIRL CAN accomplish a lot, but there are some things she couldn't do on her own. After all, it's difficult to go on a date or stage elaborate mock weddings without a man in your life. So two years after Barbie doll was introduced, it was time for her to get a boyfriend.

The first Ken dolls, straight-legged and skinny in red swim trunks, featured flocked brunette or blond hair (brownette was offered as a store exclusive). By 1962, scores of balding Ken dolls were abandoned for new painted-hair models. Ken wouldn't get "real" hair again until the 1972 Mod Hair Ken, the first with rooted hair.

Just as Mattel continued to tweak Barbie doll's appearance, the Ken doll underwent frequent, almost annual, updates.

$\mathcal{B}$ARBIE AND Ken were made for each other—starting in 1961. Here a Bubblecut Barbie and painted hair Ken wear matching Pak outfits.

NEW! FOR THE SMALL FRY!

#0524

Barbie GE-TAR™

Turn the crank, play the tune, sing the words of the Barbie song (included). Colorful, sturdy, with shoulder carrying cord. Patented musical unit. $2.00

#0750

Ken He's a doll™

Tall, crew-cut Ken makes a handsome steady for your Barbie doll. Ken is easy and fun to dress in his smartly-tailored wardrobe. Ken doll has bathing trunks, beach jacket, sandals, and a special stand to hold him upright. $3.50

We Are Family

Ken HE'S A DOLL T.M.

BARBIE'S BOYFRIEND T.M.

HE'S BARBIE'S BOYFRIEND *Ken* BY MATTEL

YOU CAN TELL IT'S **MATTEL** ...IT'S SWELL!

Ken HE'S A DOLL

BARBIE'S BOYFRIEND

HE'S BARBIE'S BOYFRIEND *Ken* BY MATTEL

*B*ARBIE DOLL'S DREAMS CAME TRUE in 1961 with the arrival of her first and only true love: Ken doll (#750). Featuring flocked blond or brunette hair, Ken came in a solid red swimsuit or a solid red with white side stripes and cork sandals with red plastic straps. A yellow terry towel came with most of the dolls, as did a red and white striped jacket.

Painted Hair Ken

W̶HILE ATTRACTIVE, THE FLOCKED hair of the first Ken doll did not hold up to strenuous play. So in 1962 Ken was released with painted blond or brunette hair representing a crewcut. Ken doll's face was also more angular and narrow. There were also a few changes to his original outfit. The swim trunks—in either red poplin or a red knit—were topped by a striped beach jacket with sewn-on terry trim. Over the years there would be other changes in store for Ken, most notably when he became more buff later in the decade.

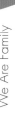

Ken's Makeover

WHEN YOU DATE BARBIE doll you had better be up for the job. Such was the pressure on 1969's New Good Lookin' Ken (#1124). Not to imply that the previous Ken dolls were somehow less than handsome, New Good Lookin' Ken just seemed a lot more hip with his brown hair, blue eyes, mustard yellow nylon short sleeve pullover and shorts in shades of red, orange and green.

Released in 1970, Talking Ken (#1111) could not only talk but when compared to the first version of Ken doll from 1961, this guy was much more muscular. That new ripped body, unfortunately, meant Ken needed new clothes. Here, he wore orange trunks and a blue and orange beach jacket. He also didn't have to worry about the ocean breezes messing his hair since it came sculpted and painted brown. Ken also had blue eyes, brown eyebrows and bendable legs.

TALKING KEN SAID:

"PJ's having a party. Let's Go."
"Have you met Barbie's new friend?"
"I'm taking the girls shopping. Want to go?"
"Put some records on and let's dance."
"I'll get the food for the party."
"Barbie's a great dancer."

MOD HAIR KEN (#4224) from 1972 was the doll's first appearance with rooted hair. Mod Ken came with only collar-length brunette hair. He was dressed in a brown-and-white checked jacket, white turtleneck dickey, tan pants and brown tennis shoes. He also came with a brown flocked sheet that could be used to add a mustache, beard and sideburns to Ken. There were two types of material types and head molds used. The smaller one is harder and the larger one is softer. There were two different box variations and three material variations used for the brown and white checkered sport coat.

SUN VALLEY KEN, released in 1974, was part of the Sports Set. Ken doll was a god medal skier in and Gold medal swimmer in 1974.

MOD HAIR Ken

with combable hair!

Beard, sideburns, 2 moustaches too!
Change them quickly!
Easily!

Change his looks for any mood
Change his style for any occasion!

NOT RECOMMENDED FOR CHILDREN UNDER 3
BECAUSE OF SMALL PARTS.

MATTEL

Released in 1980, Roller Skating Ken captured the spirit of the roller skating craze. His flashy purple jacket and short shorts also reflected the fashion sense of those Day-Glo days.

Promoted as "the doll who loves to ride horses," Horse Lovin' Ken galloped into the Barbie doll scene in 1982. Ken wore leather pants, a leather vest trimmed with fur, a red and white shirt, kerchief, boots and cowboy hat.

Earring Magic Ken, 1992

TRENDINESS WAS THE GOAL, but Earring Magic Ken doll's fashion was greatly misinterpreted at the time of release. With frosted blond hair, he wore a glitzy purple shirt and a hoop earring in his left ear. It has arguably become one of the most memorable male dolls in history. This doll was also issued for the Canadian market wearing a lavendar vest.

Allan, 1964

*K*EN GOT HIS OWN BEST FRIEND for life in 1964 when Allan (#1100) hit the scene. Allan was not only buddies with Ken but he could wear all of his clothes. Allan, who had brown painted eyes and painted, molded hair, came with blue swimming trunks, a blue, red and green striped beach jacket, and cork sandals. Allan also dated Barbie doll's best friend, Midge. Few collectors know that Allan's last name was Sherwood. Allan and Midge (Hadley) were the only married characters in the Barbie doll line.

From 1963 through 1964, Dressed Boxed Ken dolls (Box Date 1963-1964) appeared in limited quantities. These dolls came already dressed in outfits designed for Ken that could also be bought seperately. These dolls are almost impossible to find never removed from box. Released in 1963-1965, this Dressed Box Sailor Ken (#796) was set for shore leave. Ken doll's middy blouse featured authentic detailing with side zipper and a separate black cotton tie. His bell-bottomed slacks featured authentic navy styling.

Barbie's best friend Midge was available as either a redhead, blond or brunette. Pictured are a Titian, Blond (rarer version with teeth) and Brunette.

THE BEST FRIEND EVER
Midge, 1963

*B*Y 1963, THE BARBIE doll universe was expanding. Although she already possessed a blossoming wardrobe, ever-changing hairstyle and new boyfriend, Barbie doll needed a sidekick—a best friend with whom she could share secrets . . . and clothes. Enter Midge, a wide-eyed, fresh-faced and freckled counterpart to Barbie's glamour. Perky as all get-out, Midge proved a loyal and lasting best friend. By 1964, Midge doll's flippy coif was transformed to a softer pageboy, and her legs acquired a bend, updating her look slightly.

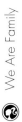

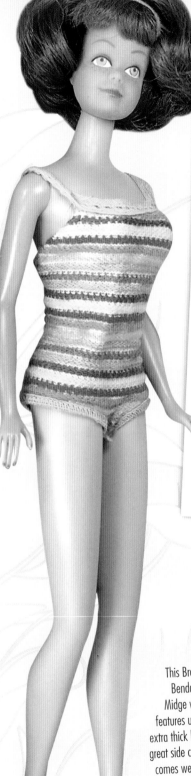

This hard-to-find, mint-in-box Midge Mix and Match Set is so scarce that there is not a lot of documentation or photos to compare it to. The set features a Brunette Midge wearing her strapless coral swimsuit. She is surrounded by great pak separates, including a black and white floral blouse, black square neck wool sweater and black full gathered cotton skirt. Her accessories include a black clutch purse, white pearl necklace and black open toe heels. The box, dated 1963, has crisp graphics in shades of lavender, pink and turquoise which show Midge wearing a floral version of Movie Date (never produced) and Sorority Meeting. The box top has a heart shaped cut out and features the Sears Department Store Logo, making it the first time a department store logo appears on a gift set.

This Brownette Bendable Leg Midge with box features unusually extra thick hair with great side curls. She comes wearing her original swimsuit and turquoise heels.

ALTHOUGH INTRODUCED AS BARBIE DOLL'S BEST FRIEND, Midge doll was only a blip on the Barbie doll map. After a few years, she disappeared from the market, only to return 20 years later in 1987 as California Midge.

Even though Midge dolls projected a perkier face to the world, Midge dolls and Barbie dolls are exactly alike aside from their heads. Original straight-legged Midge dolls had the same body and markings as Fashion Queen Barbie dolls. It's only appropriate, then, that painted hair Midge doll heads were also sold with a wig wardrobe set.

Midge Ensemble Gift Set

*T*HIS GORGEOUS MIDGE is surrounded by a whole wardrobe of Mix 'n Match knits and accessories. The long striped glittered skirt has tons of glitter. This set includes her straw hat with stripe knit band, matching striped knit purse, sash, sheath skirt, blue knit "V" top and pants, white open-toe heels and white Barbie, Ken, Midge booklet. She comes dressed in her two-piece yellow and orange swimsuit. This doll sold for $2,636 in Doll Attic's November 2006 auction.

Pink Skin Straight Leg Midge

*T*HIS DOLL CERTAINLY STANDS OUT. Midge has the Mod era pink vinyl head, and all original. Factory ribbon in hair and thick red hair in factory set. Nice pink skin vinyl on face, bright blue eyes and nice coral lips. She comes on a very rare pink skin excellent condition straight leg body which has all finger and toe polish. She is wearing a sample swimsuit never produced by Mattel. This doll sold for $936 in a May 2009 auction.

Examples of Skipper
with hair color variations
in black cherry, left,
and platinum.

BARBIE GAINS A LITTLE SISTER
Skipper, 1964

*I*NTRODUCED IN 1964 AS BARBIE DOLL'S LITTLE SISTER, Skipper was only nine inches tall, with a six-piece jointed straight-legged body, blue painted eyes and long silky hair that came in various shades of blond, brown and red. Skipper also had her own clothing line. Many of her outfits coordinated with Barbie's. Skipper came dressed in a cute solid red and red and white stripe swimsuit with white braid trim. Her accessories were red flats, a brass headband and a white comb and brush.

We Are Family

165

Dressed Box
Skipper wearing
Flower Girl outfit.

This rare Japanese Dressed Box Skipper comes wearing #1913 "Me & My Doll". Notice the Japanese issued Skipper dolls had big brown eyes versus the U.S. issued doll which had blue eyes.

SKIPPER HAS HER OWN "JUNIOR-EDITION" STYLES...THEY MATCH BARBIE'S WONDERFUL WARDROBE!

Production Sample Skipper

NEVER PRODUCED ON THE MARKET, this Malibu Skipper doll is just gorgeous with exceptionally thick saran hair, which is extra long and wavy. She comes wearing "Sound of Music" outfit which was never made available for sale. The outfit consists of a green lederhosen, red turtleneck knit top, gold braid attached to the lederhosen, matching green hat, beige knee socks and brown tennis shoes.

Francie doll World

*B*old splashy colors. Mini dresses with geometric shapes. Go-go boots. Heavily-mascaraed eyes. By the middle of the 1960s, an eruption of the attitude defined as "mod" had taken over music, makeup and fashion, so why not the toy world? While Barbie doll fashions were concurrently changing with the times, Mattel introduced another Barbie doll family member who would fully embrace the meaning of mod.

Francie doll was a true chameleon, and there was rarely a look she couldn't pull off. Released in 1966, her fashions even had names reflecting the times: Gad-Abouts, Leather Limelight, Swingin' Skimmy, Hip Knits and Fur Out. You could almost hear the go-go music in the background.

Around 1970, Francie doll's traditional hairstyle— long flippy hair with bangs—was altered on a doll that has come to be known as No Bangs Francie. This TNT doll, available in blond or brunette, featured a pulled-back hairstyle with no bangs.

Straight-leg Francie ushered in an era of splashy colors, mini dresses, go-go boots and the "mod" era into the World of Barbie.

francie™
Barbie's 'MOD'ern cousin

Francie
modeling
Japanese
Fashion.

Sun Sun Malibu Francie

A TRUE RARITY! This 1971 Sun Sun Francie was only made for the Japanese market in 1971 for a short period of time. This doll sold for $3,675 in Doll Attic's auction.

Francie Sample Doll

*M*ATTEL CREATED VARIOUS SAMPLE DOLLS that were presented as production models. This very rare Francie was one of those elusive dolls. She comes with stunning all original make up, super bright hot pink lips, and big brown eyes. Her very soft saran hair is styled in a bubblecut style. Her dress is a red velvet empire waist top with white long organza lined skirt with two red ruffle tiers near the hem. This doll sold for $4,500 at auction.

SPECIFICATION SAMPLE

Sample No. J#2

Project No. 1070 (2494)

PURPOSE OF SAMPLE

BEAUTIFUL FRANCIE wearing Japanese dress—no stock number was ever assigned to this dress.

FRANCIE JAPANESE issued ballgown FR2231.

Talking Christie, 1968

TALKING CHRISTIE (#1126) was released in 1968 to 1972 and was one of the early African-American friends of Barbie doll. She's shown here in her original light green sleeveless knit top with green and pink yarn trim at the hem. She also wore pink vinyl shorts. Her hair was issued in a soft black color and often oxidizes to red.

This Twist 'N Turn Christie (#1119) was released in 1969 in her original hot pink and yellow swimsuit. This doll has great blush on cheeks, full pink lips and long lashes, as well as reddish brown hair in a bubble type hairstyle.

The first doll in the Mattel fashion doll line to be made in the likeness of a real person was the Twiggy doll from 1967, based on the lanky British fashion model. It was a perfect addition to the "mod" era of the time.

MAKE IT REAL
Twiggy
&
TV TIES
Julia

TWIGGY™
TREASURE BOX
MATTEL INC.

FASHIONS FOR
YOUR
JULIA
DOLL
MATTEL
BY MATTEL

NEW TV STAR
DIAHANN CARROLL AS
JULIA

A notable inclusion to Mattel's multicultural family was Julia, based on the Diahann Carroll television series. Introduced in 1969, the African-American doll came dressed (among other outfits) as a nurse. Julia is pictured here wearing a very rare sample dress, never produced by Mattel.

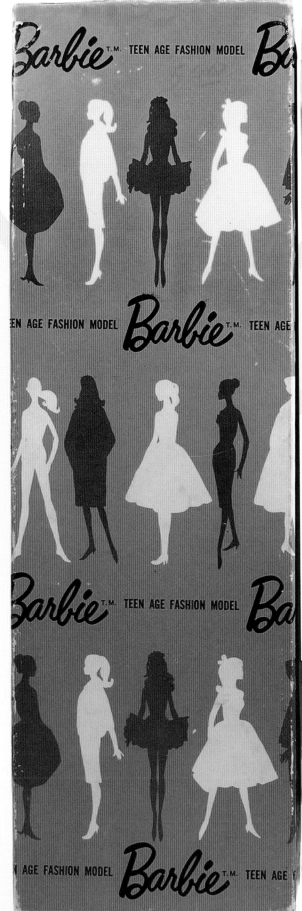

Barbie doll first demonstrated her cooking skills outdoors at her very own barbecue, and with great results. This exquisite example of a #1 Blond Ponytail Barbie in Pink Silhouette box, wearing a 1959 Barbie-Q outfit (#962), sold at a Doll Attic auction for $25,147 in 2006.

CHAPTER 10

A Rare Sight to See

The Barbie World at its Best

What would you pay for a rare Barbie doll dress? How about $5,000? That's exactly what this near-mint, incredibly rare Japanese version of the classic 1960's Let's Dance dress sold for at auction.

*B*EAUTY IS IN THE EYE OF THE BEHOLDER, it's true. Rare beauty, however, is much more measurable. Quantity or lack thereof, changes perception. We desire what is difficult to possess.

And so it is in the Barbie doll world.

During the past two decades, some of the rarest Barbie dolls and accessories have found their way into my shop. I've sold or auctioned one-of-a-kind items, prototypes, Japanese fashions, store exclusives, and items I didn't know existed until I held them in my hands. Over the years at Doll Attic, we've been blessed to feature at auction some of the finest Barbie items ever created.

Consider this: Doll Attic sold a pristine #1 Blond Ponytail Barbie doll for $25,527 in 2003. That amazing doll, which sold for $3 in 1959, still holds the world record for the highest amount ever paid for a Barbie. Three years later we sold an exquisite example of #1 Blond Ponytail Barbie in Pink Silhouette box, wearing a Barbie-Q fashion outfit for $25,147. Also in 2006, we sold one of my favorite items: a Barbie and Ken Dressed Doll Assortment store display from 1963. It was the first time I had ever seen something like this in person. That incredible display holding six dolls sold for $19,144. When you consider that the display originally sold for $70.50 you quickly realize just how passionate people can be when it comes to Barbie doll rarities.

In the following pages we showcase an exceptional array of rare dolls and accessories. Some items have survived the test of time in unparalleled condition; some were never massed produced; and others come from far-flung places. Some have sold for astounding prices, while others simply appeal to me. All, however, hold a special place in Barbie doll history.

THIS SHOWPIECE Brunette #1 Ponytail Barbie doll is a grand example of a mint-in-box beauty. She features all original makeup, a hint of smoky eye shadow, dark pointed eyebrows and awesome orangey-red lips. Time has been kind to this Barbie doll as she faded evenly to a lovely ivory color. She is complete with copper tubes in feet, original stand, booklet, heels and sunglasses. Even the box is beautiful, still bearing the $3 price sticker on an end flap. No wonder this mint-in-box Barbie doll sold for nearly $14,000 at auction.

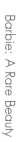

"Steel" Your Heart Away

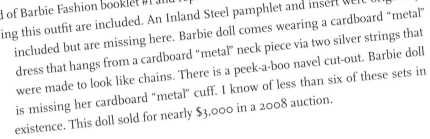

ℬARBIE DOLL COULD MAKE a potato sack look like high fashion. Need proof? Look no further than this ultra-rare Barbie doll which was part of a promotional gift set for Inland Steel Container Company circa 1967. The doll was known as "Barbie Loves Improvers" in honor of the folks at Inland Steel who were improving life through the use of aluminum and steel containers. Designer Paco Rabanne had a tough job making a glamorous outfit out of "steel" but the finished product is so very cool. The set includes a pristine Silver Ash Blond Standard Barbie doll, with bright blue side-glance eyes and a perfect pink bow in her hair. Barbie also comes packaged in a special box which has "Barbie Loves the Improvers" stamped on the outside (which doubled as the mailing box). The original liner, gold wire and clear Mod X stand and World of Barbie Fashion booklet #1 and reproduction color copy of the live model wearing this outfit are included. An Inland Steel pamphlet and insert were originally included but are missing here. Barbie doll comes wearing a cardboard "metal" dress that hangs from a cardboard "metal" neck piece via two silver strings that were made to look like chains. There is a peek-a-boo navel cut-out. Barbie doll is missing her cardboard "metal" cuff. I know of less than six of these sets in existence. This doll sold for nearly $3,000 in a 2008 auction.

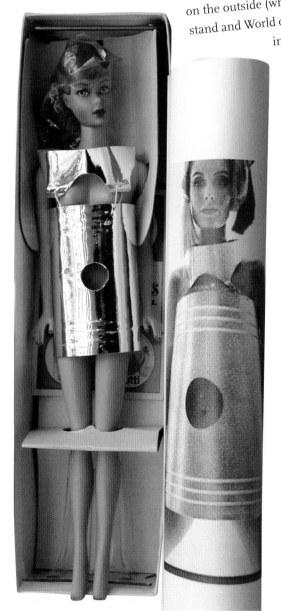

The epitome of glamour — and rarity — in Barbie doll's world, this beautiful autumn haze mink stole is one of the most desirable pieces of clothing in the doll's wardrobe. A Sear's exclusive, the stole was labeled and had a tan silk laminated lining. It came packaged in a clear box and the outer shipping box was brown corrugate cardboard. The original catalog price of $9.99 in 1964 made it the most expensive garment available. At auction, an enthusiastic collector paid more than $4,600 for it.

Ruby Red Wonder

A STAR IN ANYONE'S COLLECTION, this rare Ruby Red Variation of a Color Magic Barbie doll was once owned by a former Mattel employee. Her hair makes this doll one of the more unusual ever discovered. Although her scalp is not the painted scalp normally found on Midnight Color Magic dolls, her hair fiber is definitely the same beautiful ruby red shade that were originally on Midnight Color Magic dolls. The hairstyle makes this doll. Rooted with a center part and American Girl bangs, her hair appears to have been factory set as a nape ponytail, and curled into cluster curls. The doll's face paint is that of a blond Color Magic, with the softer makeup, light brown eye brows, lemon lips and piercing blue eyes. Wearing a mint condition Color Magic swimsuit, the doll could have been a Mattel test sample or prototype, as it has so many features of an American Girl and sports a never produced hairstyle. A rare find indeed, the doll sold for more than $2,300 at auction.

Brunette Swirl with Rare Diamond Case

YOU HAVE JUST FOUND THE pièce de résistance of Barbie doll cases: The elusive Diamond Case with window front and MOD green, blue and yellow diamond design. This case was originally only sold with a Brunette Swirl, dressed in a Fashion Queen swimsuit, and thought to be a European issued set. Some have reported the Swirls sold with this case have a fuller face. This brunette beauty has bright blue eyes and eyeliner of a 1965 American Girl and lovely peach lips. She comes wearing a Fashion Queen gold and white striped swimsuit. This case has bright graphics and window front. There is a great graphic of a Side Part American Girl on the front of the case. Inside of case has wardrobe hook. This was the only doll in the vintage era sold in a case, rather than a box.

What a Doll

*R*ARE BEAUTY COULD BE DEFINED by this spectacular doll, #6 Lemon Blond Ponytail Japanese Dressed Box Barbie doll. Wearing a Resort Set (#963) fashion outfit, this doll is simply astounding. She has a face that is stunning with perfect pinkish-coral lips, great eyebrows, sultry blue eyes and blue eyeliner. Her silky, lemon blond hair is pristine with original topknot and full, soft curly bangs. She is dressed in a complete Resort Set ensemble with charm bracelet and earrings in original cello. The red, white, and blue nautical themed outfit includes a red sailcloth jacket with middy collar, patch pockets, and white trim top, a knit navy/white horizontal striped sleeveless shell and white "cuffed" sailcloth shorts. This extremely rare doll in beautiful condition sold for more than $8,500 at auction.

The American Dream

A GORGEOUS FACTORY MINT-IN-BOX Silver-Ash Blond Side-Part American Girl Barbie doll brought $5,000 in a 2007 auction. The American Girl beauty is a wonderful example of a dazzling doll, with high color makeup and tons of blush, along with spectacular raspberry lips, bright blue eyes and brown eyebrows. Her hair remains held in place with original headband.

TNT Dynamite

AN AMAZING MOD ERA RARITY, this White Dressed Box TNT store display doll in Glimmer Glamour fashion outfit sold for more than $7,700 at auction. Not only is the doll wearing one of the rarest and most desirable Mod outfits, she is in absolutely pristine condition. It is believed the doll may have been shipped to display case manufacturers to be fastened into retail display units, which were then shipped to retailers. It is suggested that Mattel created some overstocks of these white boxed dolls that were never attached to display cases and were later sold in the Mattel company store. This doll may be one such extra display doll as she was obviously never removed from her white box. The box resembles a vintage Barbie doll box but has no graphics. She is attached to the box with ivory colored plastic coated wire. The doll is absolutely exquisite. She has beautiful champagne hued hair in its original set with orange bow and factory cello on head. Her face is perfect, with lots of blush, un-faded vinyl, perfect lashes and rosy lips. She comes wearing a pristine Glimmer Glamour ensemble which is quite elusive in part because the delicate fabrics do not wear well. The dress was lined in blue silk and the sheer organdy overskirt and over-blouse featured golden glitter dots. This organdy is extremely fragile. Golden braid accented the bottom of the bodice and a wide goldtone belt nipped in the waist. The coat was a trapeze style with a tie at the neck and ¾ sleeves. The fabric was a golden lamé knit lined in yellow nylon. Butterscotch color hose (exclusive to this set) and clear open-toe heels with golden glitter completed this outfit. Her wristband is also not the typical Barbie doll wrist tag of the era, but a silver foil band that reads "Made in Japan" on both the front and the back.

$\mathcal{A}$ STUNNING EXAMPLE of a European version of a Platinum Swirl Ponytail Barbie, this factory mint doll came dressed in the Fashion Queen swimsuit. The doll's face features striking eyes and lovely, perfectly white lips. Her gorgeous "white-look" platinum blond hair is soft and shiny in the original ponytail. Her Midge/Barbie doll body is just terrific with great coral finger and toe polish. She comes with her original gold wrist tag, gold wire stand, booklet and heels in original cello. In never removed from box condition, she sold for nearly $3,000 at auction in 2007.

$\mathcal{A}$ TRANSITIONAL DOLL, this Platinum Swirl American Girl Barbie doll is a beautiful example of a rarity produced in 1965. Mattel used the beautiful Swirl ponytail head on a Bent Leg American Girl body and packaged them in the American Girl box, marked "Plat. Pony" on the end flap. This untouched Barbie doll has perfect platinum hair with original ribbon and bobby pin held in place with factory cello. Her lovely face has bright white lips and piercing blue eyes. She comes on a factory mint body complete with finger and toe polish and comes wearing her American Girl swimsuit and mint tag on wrist. Includes copper stand, original booklet and heels in cello and earrings are in a separate baggie. This doll was never removed from box and still carried the original price sticker of $3.79. She sold at auction for considerably more: $4,500.

$\mathscr{T}$HIS FACTORY MINT, Platinum TNT Stacey is wearing a prototype outfit, making her coveted by collectors. While Stacey is exquisite with mint hair, long, lush lashes, dark pink lips and blush on cheeks, it's her outfit that really stands out. She comes wearing a never produced, one-of-a-kind "Stripes are Happening" outfit. This set has a red faux suede top, with brass ring closures, instead of the pink vinyl top which was produced. Her matching skirt also has the red faux suede waistband. The set includes her matching striped knee socks, striped sleeveless shell and yellow ankle boots.

$\mathscr{T}$HIS IS A STORE DISPLAY TNT Blond Short Flip Stacey. Sassy Stacey is wearing a mint "Lovely Sleep-Ins" outfit with perfect wrist tag. Factory mint face has beautiful blush and gorgeous lashes. This doll sold for $525 at auction.

$\mathcal{A}$ TRULY RARE FIND, this is a Japanese Dressed Box Platinum Stacey never removed from box wearing an extremely rare outfit: a lime green cotton knit suit, trimmed in off-white satin, green belt and satin sleeveless blouse with three lime green buttons and matching skirt. Also included is a matching white felt hat trimmed in green rik rak and green satin bow. Accessories include closed green heels, green and white shoulder purse, pink eyelash brush in package, Mod White X Stand and red round plastic disc that attaches to the X Stand for Stacey to sit. Stacey has hair in factory perfect set, with thick untouched spit curls, red bow in ponytail, and original plastic band in middle of ponytail. Her face is exceptional with bright eyes, full lips, blush, luscious lashes and great color. Dressed Box Japanese dolls seldom show up for auction, which adds to the hard-to-find nature of this spectacular doll, which sold for $4,830 in 2004 sale.

Carnation Doll

*T*HIS VERY SPECIAL PROMOTIONAL DOLL was offered as a premium prize by the Carnation Company in 1964-1965. Customers could send in one Carnation malted milk label with cash to receive a special Barbie doll or outfit. In 1964 customers could select either a Barbie or a Midge doll and a number of different outfits. In 1965 the choices were expanded to include Allan, Ken and Skipper dolls as well. This stunning doll has factory mint hair in original bands and nice full bangs. She comes wearing original red swimsuit and perfect gold foil wrist tag on wrist. Includes special "Carnation Barbie and Midge" booklet, Exclusive Fashion Booklet #1 and red open-toe heels sealed in factory cello. Also included, which is exclusive to these dolls, is the small fold out Carnation Booklet which shows which toys are available with this special offer.

$\mathcal{O}$NE OF THE RAREST DOLLS of the Mod Era, this European Dressed Box TNT Platinum Barbie doll has never been removed from box. Her high-color makeup is stunning and bright. Note the blush on cheeks and bright blue eyes, long lashes and full red lips. Her gorgeous white hair is in the original set with bright pink ribbon in ponytail. Barbie doll is wearing a "Learning to Ride" outfit. A real doll, she sold for almost $3,000 at auction.

$\mathcal{D}$ISCRIMINATING COLLECTORS SWOONED over this never-removed-from-box Redhead TNT in Japanese fashion. A European exclusive Barbie, these dolls were packaged without accessories and came in a distinctive blister card packaging with hot pink label on the front of the clear top. This stunner has gleaming red hair, with hot pink hair ribbon. She also has a gorgeous high color face with full lashes and perfect pink vinyl skin. She comes smartly dressed in a beautiful Japanese exclusive suit (#2628), which consists of a two-piece tailored red and white checked cotton suit, and orange bow heels. You will notice the $2.25 price tag remains on this superb doll that sold for almost $3,700 at auction.

Japanese Beauty

THIS FACTORY MINT JAPANESE Dressed Box Side Part Bubblecut Barbie is a rare piece of history. She comes wearing a mint Japanese silver and black kimono, with obi in excellent condition. Accessories include the ultra rare Japanese Barbie doll pedestal stand which has Barbie by Mattel written in gold on the pedestal base, Japanese fashion booklet, original cardboard neck brace and Japanese issued pink lamé purse.

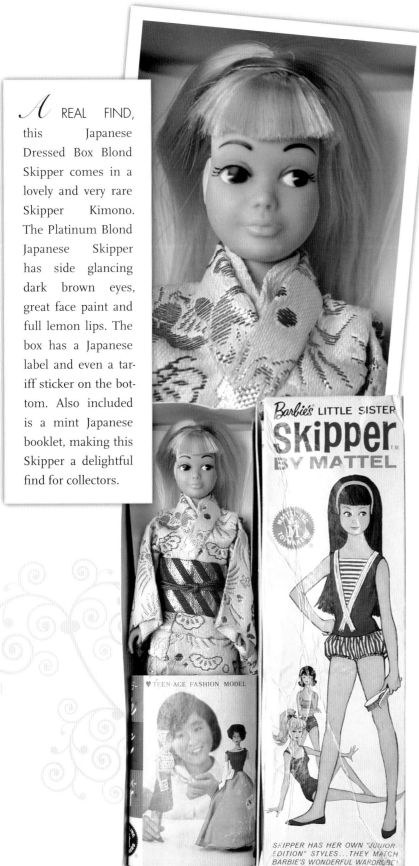

A REAL FIND, this Japanese Dressed Box Blond Skipper comes in a lovely and very rare Skipper Kimono. The Platinum Blond Japanese Skipper has side glancing dark brown eyes, great face paint and full lemon lips. The box has a Japanese label and even a tariff sticker on the bottom. Also included is a mint Japanese booklet, making this Skipper a delightful find for collectors.

JAPANESE MIDGE MINT IN BOX. This Japanese Midge is made of a completely different face mold than those in the U.S.; she has a unique gentle expression with her sultry brown eyes and small coral lips. She has the brown molded hair much like the Fashion Queen doll marketed in the U.S., with blue band in hair and brunette wig. She is wearing a hard-to-find Silver Kimono with a black and silver obi.

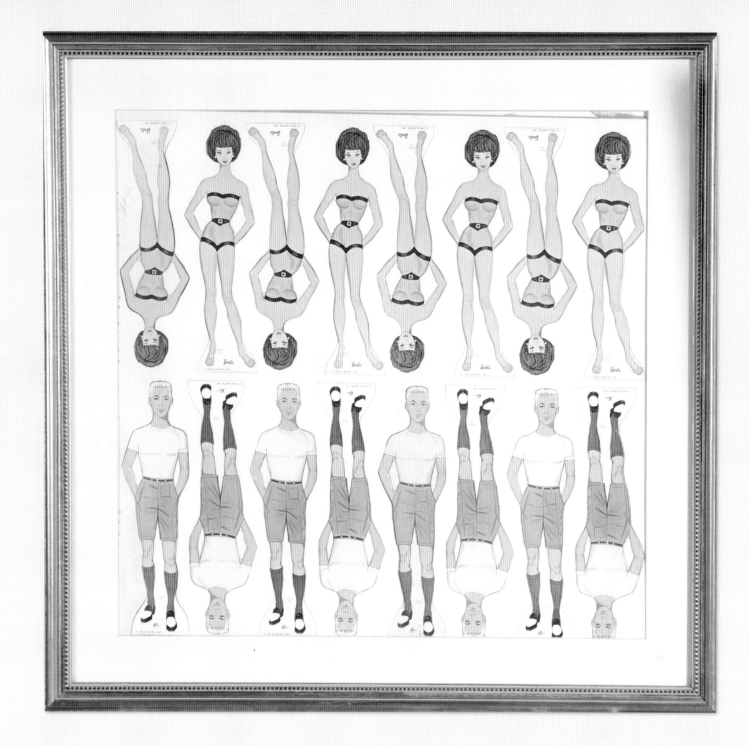

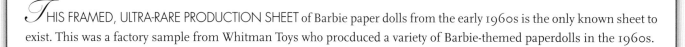

*T*HIS FRAMED, ULTRA-RARE PRODUCTION SHEET of Barbie paper dolls from the early 1960s is the only known sheet to exist. This was a factory sample from Whitman Toys who procduced a variety of Barbie-themed paperdolls in the 1960s.

THIS #2 BLOND PONYTAIL
Barbie doll features full, deep
red lips, dark pointed stenciled
eyebrows and sultry white eyes
with great blue eyeliner. She has
pretty, soft, full bangs. Mint in
box condition, the doll sold for
$5,800 at auction.

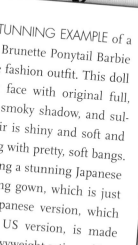

THIS IS A STUNNING EXAMPLE of a
mint-in-box #4 Brunette Ponytail Barbie
doll in Japanese fashion outfit. This doll
has a gorgeous face with original full,
red lips, lots of smoky shadow, and sultry eyes. Her hair is shiny and soft and
very full and long with pretty, soft bangs.
She comes wearing a stunning Japanese
Enchanted Evening gown, which is just
exquisite. The Japanese version, which
differs from the US version, is made
from a thicker heavyweight satin and has
a red rose accent at hip. Note the Japanese
Fashion Booklet included with the doll.

Orange Blossom Special

𝒥APANESE DRESSED BOX BRUNETTE BUBBLECUT Orange Blossom (#987) is in mint condition. Discriminating collectors will flip for this fabulous rare find! This raven haired bubblecut Barbie doll features vibrant facepaint, turquoise eyes and eyeliner. Her beautiful big red lips are all original.

This Dressed Box beauty includes a Japanese fashion booklet and very rare Japanese pedestal stand, with the Barbie logo embossed in gold on pedestal base. This doll sold for $5,000 in a 2007 auction.

A Dream Come True

STRIKING IN THE 1963 BRIDE'S DREAM fashion outfit (#947), this lovely Dressed Box Titian Up-Do Ponytail Barbie doll would make any groom blush. This stunning white satin, short-sleeved wedding dress featured a full overskirt with tiered ruffle front panel in soft chiffon. A tiny bow at the waist was a delicate accent. Some of the accessories were the same as those included with 1959's Wedding Day (#972). They included: tulle veil with "pearl" head piece, open-toe white heels, blue garter, fabric flower lace base bouquet and white satin streamers, and graduated "pearl" necklace. However, the gloves with Bride's Dream were elbow length. The doll sold for $1,260 at a 2005 auction.

ONE OF THE MORE BEAUTIFUL DOLLS to come through the Doll Attic, this #2 Blond Ponytail Barbie doll has mesmerizing face paint, with full orange lips, nicely stenciled brows, soft blush and incredible eye. The factory-original blue eyeliner is enhanced by a line of pink shadow topped with smoky grey shadow, giving Barbie doll's eyes a very Technicolor look. Her hair is a golden blond with nice full bangs and restyled ponytail, with hard curl on bottom ponytail. She comes wearing her black and white swimsuit and original hoop earrings. This fetching beauty brought more than $6,000 at auction.

CONSIDERED BY BARBIE EXPERTS as the rarest of all the Bubblecut hair colors, this Brownette Bubblecut Barbie doll is stunning. There's not a hair out of place. Her face paint is striking, with dark brown eyebrows, smoky eye shadow and juicy red lips. Wearing her original black and white striped swimsuit, Barbie doll also comes with a booklet, sunglasses and heels, as well as a black wire stand. This spectacular doll sold for $1,400 at a 2006 auction.

A Rare Sight to See

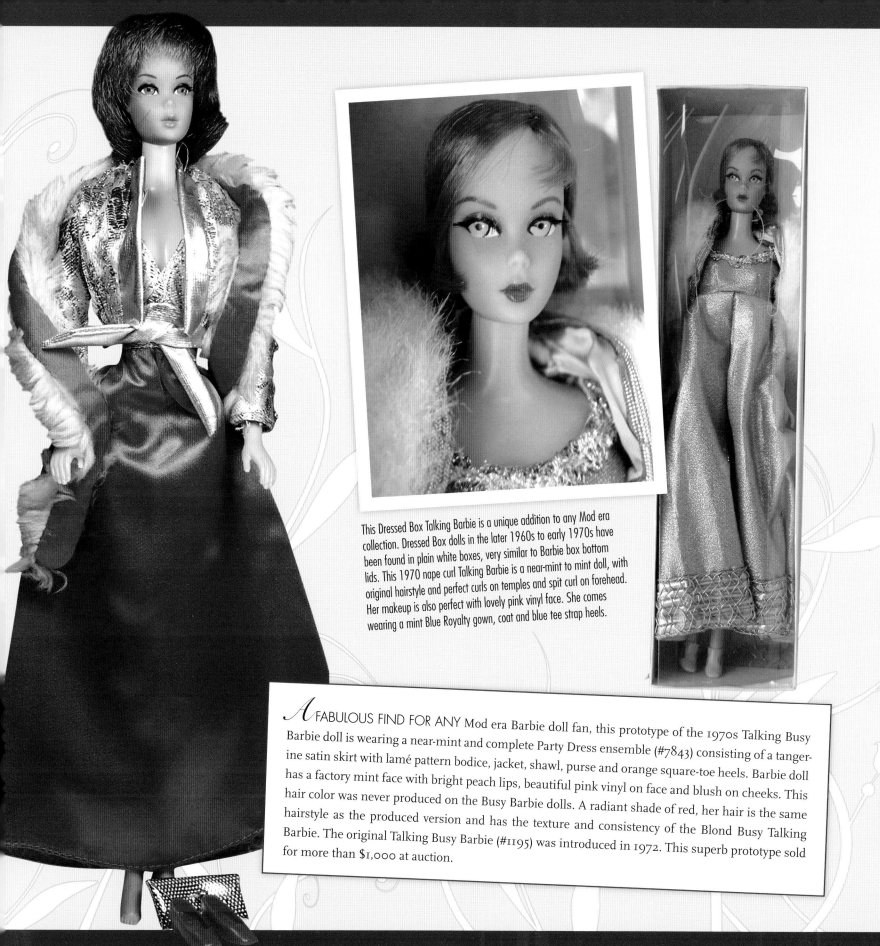

This Dressed Box Talking Barbie is a unique addition to any Mod era collection. Dressed Box dolls in the later 1960s to early 1970s have been found in plain white boxes, very similar to Barbie box bottom lids. This 1970 nape curl Talking Barbie is a near-mint to mint doll, with original hairstyle and perfect curls on temples and spit curl on forehead. Her makeup is also perfect with lovely pink vinyl face. She comes wearing a mint Blue Royalty gown, coat and blue tee strap heels.

A FABULOUS FIND FOR ANY Mod era Barbie doll fan, this prototype of the 1970s Talking Busy Barbie doll is wearing a near-mint and complete Party Dress ensemble (#7843) consisting of a tangerine satin skirt with lamé pattern bodice, jacket, shawl, purse and orange square-toe heels. Barbie doll has a factory mint face with bright peach lips, beautiful pink vinyl on face and blush on cheeks. This hair color was never produced on the Busy Barbie dolls. A radiant shade of red, her hair is the same hairstyle as the produced version and has the texture and consistency of the Blond Busy Talking Barbie. The original Talking Busy Barbie (#1195) was introduced in 1972. This superb prototype sold for more than $1,000 at auction.

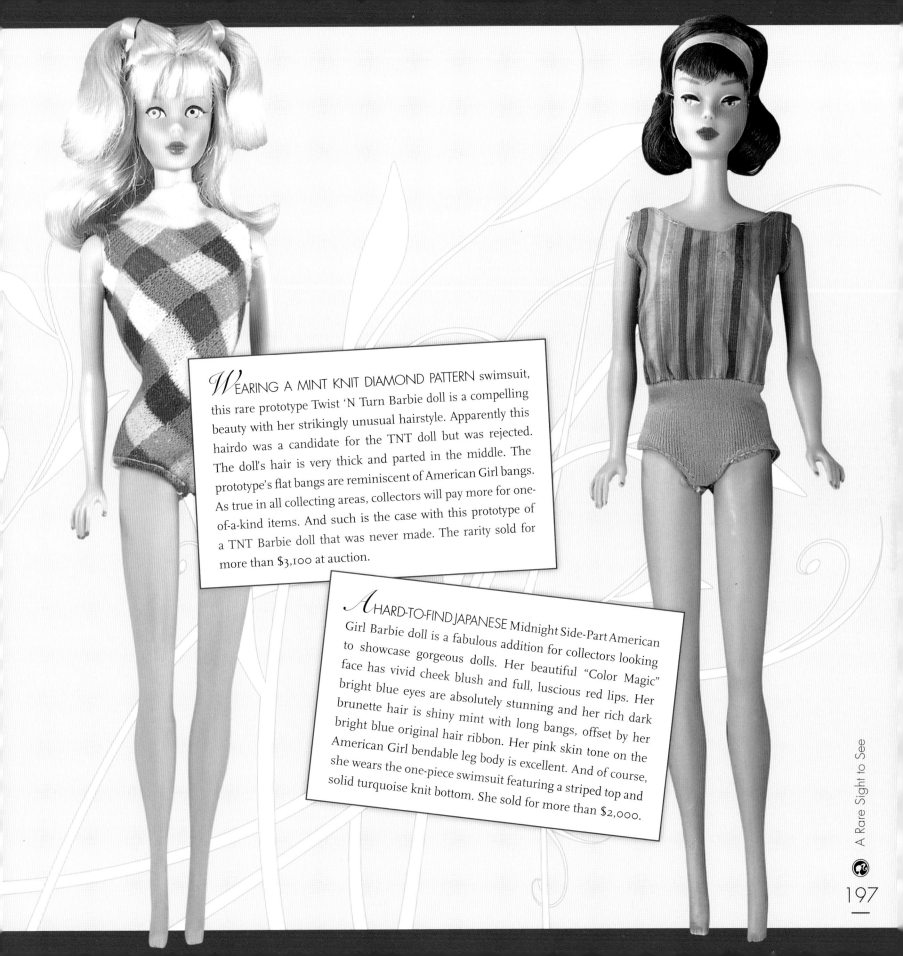

$\mathcal{W}$EARING A MINT KNIT DIAMOND PATTERN swimsuit, this rare prototype Twist 'N Turn Barbie doll is a compelling beauty with her strikingly unusual hairstyle. Apparently this hairdo was a candidate for the TNT doll but was rejected. The doll's hair is very thick and parted in the middle. The prototype's flat bangs are reminiscent of American Girl bangs. As true in all collecting areas, collectors will pay more for one-of-a-kind items. And such is the case with this prototype of a TNT Barbie doll that was never made. The rarity sold for more than $3,100 at auction.

$\mathcal{A}$ HARD-TO-FIND JAPANESE Midnight Side-Part American Girl Barbie doll is a fabulous addition for collectors looking to showcase gorgeous dolls. Her beautiful "Color Magic" face has vivid cheek blush and full, luscious red lips. Her bright blue eyes are absolutely stunning and her rich dark brunette hair is shiny mint with long bangs, offset by her bright blue original hair ribbon. Her pink skin tone on the American Girl bendable leg body is excellent. And of course, she wears the one-piece swimsuit featuring a striped top and solid turquoise knit bottom. She sold for more than $2,000.

*W*ITH A FACE TO DIE FOR, this #1 Brunette Ponytail Barbie doll is stunning with deep red lips, gorgeous blush, hand-painted eyebrows and sultry white eyes. Her lovely dark hair is nice and long, in the original set with hard curl. She comes dressed in her original black and white swimsuit and includes #1 black heels, sunglasses, and hoop earrings. This mint-in-box Barbie doll sold for $6,350 in a 2006 auction.

N A PINK SILHOUETTE
Dressed Box, this #3 Ponytail
Barbie doll is stunning in a
mint condition "Solo in the
Spotlight" fashion outfit. But
what makes her extremely
rare is the factory bun in
her ponytail. She also has
perfect ringlet curls on her
bangs. The doll has perfect
makeup, vibrant blue eyeliner,
dark brown eyebrows, smoky
shadow on eyes and deep red
lips. This eye-popping beauty
sold for more than $5,500 at a
2007 auction.

Sample Superstar Barbie in Sample Outfit

A GEM FROM THE EARLY SUPERSTAR DAYS, this hand-painted beauty has a one-of-a-kind hairstyle with tons of curls pulled back into a ponytail and cute bangs framing her face. She has brilliant turquoise eyes and that great Superstar smile which ushered in a new era for Barbie doll in the mid 1970s. She comes on a Ballerina body and is modeling a fabulous "Debbie Reynolds" style dress. The fabric is a taffeta aqua and white gingham, with a white eyelet bodice insert, embellished with three rhinestones and aqua velvet brow at waist. Her coat is made of an aqua fleece with a portrait collar and an aqua chiffon scarf.

Prototype TNT Barbie

*T*HIS DOLL CAPTURES THE MOMENT IN TIME when Mattel updated Barbie from the American Girl to the Mod TNT Barbie doll. This head mold was a pre-production TNT/ Standard face and is believed to be the last experimental head mold before the finalization of the TNT doll. This doll has a hand-painted face with pink lips, blue eyes with blue liner and auburn brows and does not have rooted eyelashes. Her head vinyl is extremely pliable and there is no rooting for hair. Instead, she comes with a blond flip wig. She comes wearing "Fashion Bouquet" dress with vinyl belt, white open-toe heels and a Mod X stand.

A Rare Sight to See

Japanese Exclusives

ONE OF THE MOST INTRIGUING THINGS about Barbie doll collecting is finding those rare items, or items you never knew existed. Japanese Exclusives fascinate collectors for that very reason because none of these items were ever offered for sale in the United States. So for many collectors, Japanese Exclusives open up an entirely new world of mystery and enchantment. The dolls and fashions captivate collectors and often fuel their passion to find more. The differences between Japanese-issued items and U.S.-issued are unique and even somewhat subtle, but remain for many the "holy grail" in Barbie collecting. These Japanese variations, be it in the form of fabric or embellishments, make displaying U.S. and Japanese variations side-by-side visually fascinating and great fun.

Barbie Japanese fashion #2100-2613.

Francie Japanese fashion #DS 2232.

The bright and sassy, hard-to-find Japanese polka dot version of After Five outfit is very rare. This dress is made out of a heavy cotton fabric, with red, orange and green polka dots. There are four large buttons on bodice. It has the same organza collar as the US issued After Five outfit. The outfit includes a pearl necklace, red clutch and red open-toe heels.

Francie Japanese fashion #DS 2240.

#1022 Barbie
Pep Rally.

A Gift for the Ages

GIFT SETS HAVE LONGED BEEN CHERISHED by fans of Barbie doll. In the 1990s, many of the sets were expensive and marketed to and for adult collectors. But in the 1960s they were strictly child's play. Today these early gift sets are not only valuable but rekindle memories of an innocent time when the most important thing in the world was playing with your dolls.

#892 Barbie & Ken Gift Set.

4 DRESSED DOLLS INCLUDED:
BARBIE IN "BRIDES DREAM"
KEN® IN TUXEDO
MIDGE™ IN "ORANGE BLOSSOM™"
SKIPPER™ IN "FLOWER GIRL"

All of BARBIE's teen-age fashion model clothes fit Miss BARBIE, MIDGE and
FASHION QUEEN® BARBIE. All of KEN's clothes fit ALLAN.

Barbie's
TEEN-AGE FASHION MODEL
WEDDING PARTY GIFT SET
BY MATTEL

YOU CAN TELL IT'S **MATTEL**...IT'S SWELL!

*B*ARBIE HAS ALWAYS made a beautiful bride and this never-removed-from box Barbie Wedding Gift Set (1964-1965#1017)illustrates why. This incredible set is in near mint condition and complete. But what makes the set so desirable are the gorgeous dolls found inside. Included are a fantastic platinum blond Bubblecut Barbie doll surrounded by her incredible wedding party: brunette Skipper in Flower Girl outfit, titian Midge in Orange Blossom outfit, and brunette Ken in Tuxedo. If you look close, you can see the little gold ring in place on the pillow. All dolls have their wrist tags intact and the bright orange liner is mint with the cellophane still around it.

#1010 'Round the Clock Gift Set.

#1018 Barbie & Ken Little Theatre Gift Set.

Complete with Talking Barbie doll, bendable legs, real eyelashes, pink satin coat, pink/white tiered dress, pink panty hose, satin purse, gold gloves, shoes, hanger, swimsuit

Talk of the Town

A COMPLETE 1970S TALKING BARBIE Pink Premier Set, with Talking Barbie doll, bendable legs, pink satin coat with gold collar, matching satin and pleated white nylon dress, hot pink pantyhose, satin and gold purse, gold gloves and hot pink pilgrim heels is a real find. A JC Penney exclusive, the set includes a mint-in-box Blond Talking Barbie doll with hair ribbons, bright pink full lips and tad of blush on her cheeks. Note the perfect wrist tag. This set sold for nearly $900 at auction.

The Hostess worth the Mostest

*W*HEN BARBIE ENTERTAINS, collectors pay attention—especially when it comes to the vintage, never-removed-from-box 1965 Barbie's Hostess Set (#1034). The set includes many easy-to-lose pieces, making this never-removed-from-box set extremely valuable to collectors. The original price tag reads $6.88 on the box, but this pristine find, with its 46-piece Cook 'N Serve set and two fashion ensembles, sold for nearly $9,000 at auction.

The Francie and Casey Fashion Boutique Store Displays features: Brunette Casey in Gold Rush outfit; Blond short Flip Francie in Land Ho outfit; Brunette Short Flip Francie in Tennis Tunic; and Platinum Blond Casey in Something Else outfit. This display sold for more than $2,300 at auction.

One of the rarer finds in Barbie collecting, 1968's The World of Barbie Store Display features: Blond Flip Francie in Night Blooms fashion outfit; Brunette Casey in Culotte Wot? fashion; Brunette Casey in Pazaam fashion; and Blond Francie in Tenterrific. This hard-to-find display sold for $5,250 at auction.

Barbie Store Displays

*B*ARBIE STORE DISPLAYS ARE TRUE BARBIE RARITIES, never intended to be sold to customers. These displays were used as tools to attract customers to Barbie doll and her beautiful fashions.

This dazzling Barbie and Stacey Fashion Boutique features: Light Brown Talking Barbie doll in Fab City; Platinum Blond Talking Stacey in Let's Have a Ball; Redhead TNT Stacey in Made for Each Other; and Brownette TNT Barbie in Winter Wedding.

Barbie® AND Ken® BY MATTEL

BARBIE'S AND KEN'S COMPLETE FASHION WARD

Original Mattel Logo only available to toy stores.

MATTEL KEY DEALER · NEW TOY HEADQUARTERS ·
M

ORIGINALLY MARKETED by Mattel to retailers, this is an eye-catching Barbie and Ken Dressed Doll Assortment store display (#909) from 1963. An incredible piece, the display originally sold as two units, with six dolls in each unit. Each unit was an easel-backed 16" x 31" corrugated display that held six dolls and originally sold for $70.50. The availability of this item was limited. The dolls came in distinctive striped boxes with acetate cover and were pre-priced for resale. What many collectors do not realize is the outfit label appearing on the end flap included a perforated price tag. Mattel intended retailers to sell these boxed dolls and reorder to refill their displays. From top row, left to right: #6 Redhead Ponytail dressed in Garden Party fashion outfit; Ken in Time for Tennis outfit; Ash Blond Bubblecut Barbie doll wears a Nighty Negligee. On the bottom row (from left): Brunette Bubblecut Barbie doll dressed in American Airlines fashion outfit; Ken in Casuals outfit, a painted hair brunette doll in pristine condition, including car keys in booklet cello; and blond Bubblecut Barbie doll dressed in Mood for Music fashion outfit.

In all my years of collecting this is the first time that I have had the privilege of seeing this incredible piece of Barbie history in person. This rare store display brought $19,144 in a 2006 auction.

A Rare Sight to See

211

Barbie
Picture Frame
Pendant Radio.

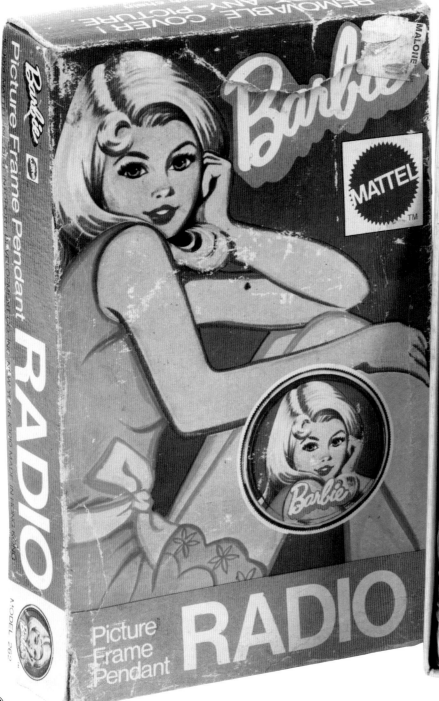

CHAPTER 11

For the Love of Licensing

Barbie Licensed Products

JUST A FEW YEARS AFTER BARBIE doll graced store shelves, products bearing her unmistakable image were being produced and, in turn, snatched up by eager buyers. Many licensed products were simply extensions of the Barbie play ethic—that included cases in which to store the dolls, toy vehicles and hair play/role play items (such as toy jewelry and vanity sets). Other companies licensed the Barbie name and image to use on apparel, including everything from shirts to tennis shoes.

It is believed that one of the earliest licensees was Standard Plastic Products in the 1960s. The company, often referred to as SPP, was well known for its vinyl wallets, binders, pouches, pencil cases, doll cases and other accessories. The pieces were often made of glossy black vinyl decorated with colorful silhouetted images. Cases branched out to include different sizes, shapes, colors and styles—and some were made for other members of Barbie's family, including Ken, Skipper and Midge.

Another early licensee that made a huge impact was American Greetings. In 1963, the company obtained a license to produce Barbie illustrated products, including napkins, greeting cards, paper plates, table covers and party centerpieces. Such disposable pieces brought Barbie to the forefront of little girls' birthday parties—fully solidifying the bond between little girls and their favorite doll. Other companies—such as House of Paper and Whitman—soon attained licenses for other Barbie paper products, and there hasn't been a decade since that hasn't been plastered with Barbie paper goods in one form or another.

While some licensed products fared better than others, one of the undisputed successes over the years was the partnership of Mattel and Hallmark. In 1992, the greeting card company teamed with Mattel to produce its first Barbie Christmas ornament; it would replicate the 1993 Happy Holidays Barbie. Almost 20 years later, the line continues and has created many miniature variations of the doll.

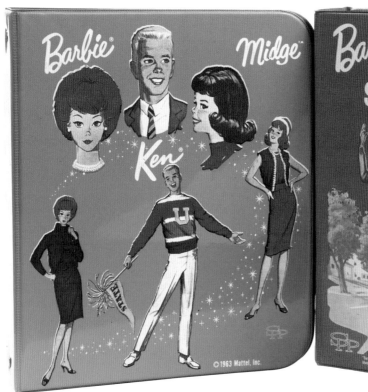
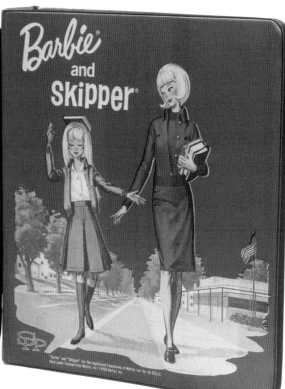

Barbie made going to school stylish and fun with these vibrant three-ring binders produced by Standard Plastic Products.

The beige version of Barbie's Own Sportscar in original packaging is a prototype and the only one known to exist. The car was produced by Irwin Products in 1962.

Barbie hit the water in her very own speedboat made by Irwin Corporation, 1964.

Vintage Barbie doll clocks.

Barbie Play Ring promised every little girl could have "a touch of glamour" in their live. And for only 29 cents!

Does anyone really know what time it is?
They do if they have this Barbie watch set which featured one watch and three watch bands.

Canadian issued Ken vinyl case.

Canadian issued Barbie vinyl case.

Skipper
Purse Pal.

Skipper and Skooter
carrying case.

Barbie Carry-All.

Francie
carrying
case.

Barbie goes Traveling Carrying Case.

The Barbie Play Hat
was produced by Benay-
Albee in 1962.

Barbie Pretty Up Time featured a mirror, brush and comb.

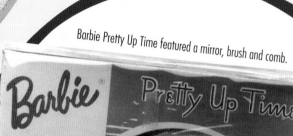

Sew your own *Ken* doll wardrobe!

MATTEL, INC. TOYMAKERS

HE'S Barbie's BOY FRIEND

Ken

HE'S A DOLL

WARDROBE PATTERNS

by MATTEL

Easy to follow patterns and instructions.

6 *new designs for* *Ken*

Barbie **Pretty Up Time**

- **MIRROR**
- **BRUSH**
- **COMB**

BALLERINA

Barbie

GROUP E
6 PATTERNS
60¢

MATTEL, INC. TOYMAKERS

Ken HE'S A DOLL
BARBIE'S BOYFRIEND

v-Easy *patterns* by ADVANCE

GROUP E
6 PATTERNS
75¢

Ken HE'S A DOLL!
BARBIE'S BOYFRIEND

v-Easy *patterns* by ADVANCE

Genuine *Ken* doll patterns

Genuine Ken doll wardrobe patterns
provided easy-to-follow instructions
for six outfits for Barbie's boyfriend.

Barbie's Letter Box, produced by Montac, featured paper, envelopes and an application to the Barbie Fan Club. If you have to write a note, what better way than with Barbie stationery?

Barbie Greeting Cards provided the perfect wishes for birthdays and Valentine's Day.

Canadian issued Barbie book bags.

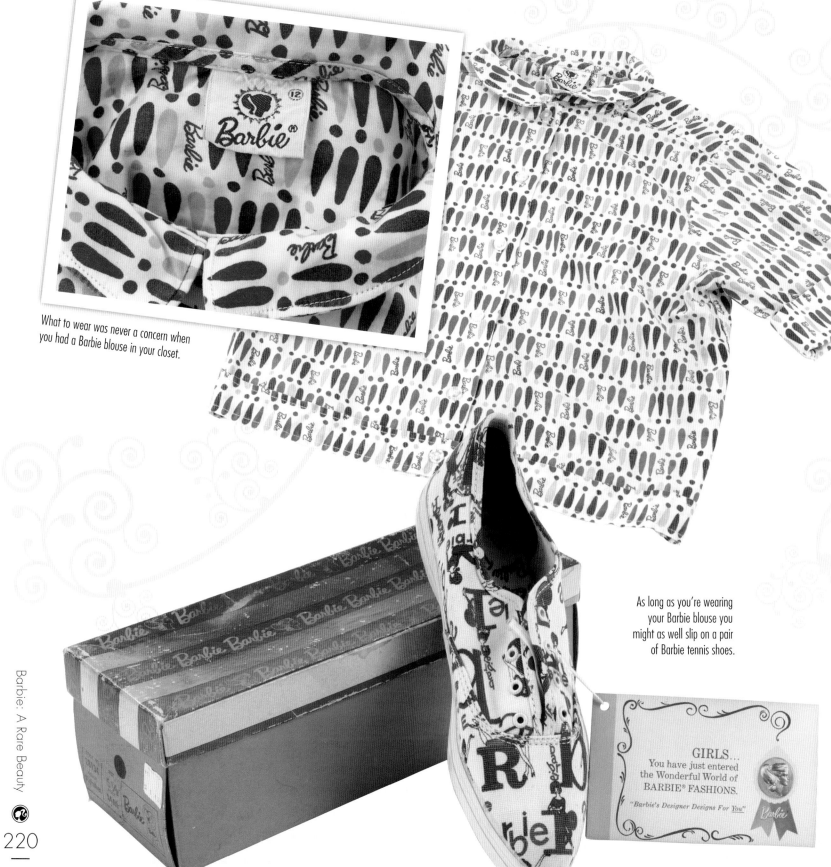

What to wear was never a concern when you had a Barbie blouse in your closet.

As long as you're wearing your Barbie blouse you might as well slip on a pair of Barbie tennis shoes.

GIRLS...
You have just entered the Wonderful World of BARBIE® FASHIONS.

"Barbie's Designer Designs For You"

Playing doctor was never more fun than with your very own Ken Doctor Kit, especially with the help of nurse Barbie and nurse Skipper, all produced by Pressman.

Halloween was frighteningly beautiful when you could dress up in your very own Barbie costume.

Barbie Magic Window allowed children to color on the "Magic Window" and then erase and color another picture.

Bibliography

BOOKS

Blitman, Joe; Barbie and Her Mod, Mod, Mod, Mod World of Fashion; Hobby House Press, Grantsville, Maryland, 1996

D'Amato, Jennie; Barbie: All Dolled Up (Celebrating 50 Years of Barbie); Running Press, Philadelphia, Pennsylvania, 2009

Deutsch, Stefanie; Barbie: The First 30 Years – 1959 through 1989; Collector Books, Paducah, Kentucky, 1996

Eames, Sarah Sink; Barbie Fashion Volume I, 1959-1967; Collector Books, Paducah, Kentucky, 1990

Fennick, Janine; The Collectible Barbie Doll, second edition; Courage Books, Philadelphia, Pennsylvania, 1999

Handler, Ruth, with Jacqueline Shannon; Dream Doll: The Ruth Handler Story; Longmeadow Press, Stamford, Connecticut, 1994

Korbeck, Sharon; The Best of Barbie: Four Decades of the World's Favorite Doll; Krause Publications, 2001

Melillo, Marcie; The Ultimate Barbie Doll Book; Krause Publications, Iola, Wisconsin, 1997

WEB SITES

Barbie Collector, www.barbiecollector.com, Mattel Inc.

Fashion Doll Guide, www.fashion-doll-guide.com

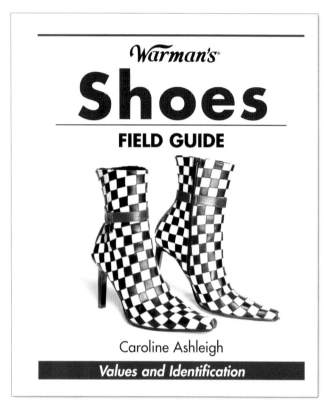
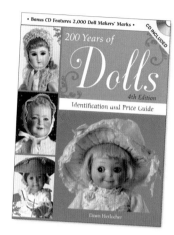

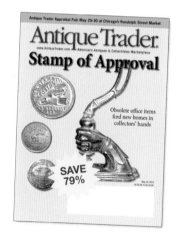